Adventure Stories for Reading, Learning and Literacy

Cross-curricular resources for the primary school

Mal Leicester and
Roger Twelvetrees

Illustrations by Apsley

Routledge
Taylor & Francis Group

LONDON AND NEW YORK

This edition first published 2010
by Routledge
2 Park Square, Milton Park, Abingdon, Oxon, OX14 4RN

Simultaneously published in the USA and Canada
by Routledge
270 Madison Avenue, New York, NY 10016

Routledge is an imprint of the Taylor & Francis Group, an informa business

Typeset in Bembo by Prepress Ptojects Ltd, Perth, UK
Printed and bound in Great Britain by TJ International Ltd, Padstow, Cornwall

British Library Cataloguing in Publication Data
A catalogue record for this book is available from the British Library

Library of Congress Cataloging-in-Publication Data
Leicester, Mal.
Adventure stories for reading, learning, and literacy : cross-curricular resources for the
primary school / Mal Leicester and Roger Twelvetrees.
p. cm.
1. Reading (Elementary) 2. Reading. 3. Literacy programs. 4. Literature—Study and
teaching (Elementary) I. Twelvetrees, Roger. II. Title.
LB1573.L425 2010
379.2'4—dc22
2009053226

ISBN10: 0-415-55995-2 (hbk)
ISBN10: 0-415-55996-0 (pbk)
ISBN10: 0-203-84911-6 (ebk)

ISBN13: 978-0-415-55995-9 (hbk)
ISBN13: 978-0-415-55996-6 (pbk)
ISBN13: 978-0-203-84911-8 (ebk)

A**...... ....** eading,
L**.......**

Adventure Stories for Reading, Learning and Literacy takes a unique approach to cross-curricular teaching in the primary classroom. Providing eight original adventure stories, the authors build up a suite of resources and activities for teachers to use in the classroom, providing cross-curricular links in line with the PNS framework to literacy, science, PE, design and technology, numeracy, geography and history. Though the stories will interest both girls and boys, they take special .... achieve less highly than girls in reading

.... and social values, and can be used .... initiatives in primary schools. With .... s book offers instant ideas which can be implemented easily in teachers' plans and in the classroom and assembly, and will appeal to all busy teachers, NQTs and teachers in training.

Mal Leicester is Professor Emeritus at Nottingham University, based in the School of Education.

Roger Twelvetrees is an engineer and a children's author.

Contents

Acknowledgements

We are grateful to Bruce Roberts for his patience and for several helpful suggestions. We also wish to acknowledge Inky Fingers Publishers (twelvetrees@ mac.com) for use of adapted stories from their Cosy Park Garage Series.

Introduction

The power of story as a hook into learning

It is known that boys are less readily hooked into reading and the world of books than are girls. We hope that both boys and girls will enjoy the child-friendly material presented in this book.

The power of story has been used in each of Mal Leicester's previous collections of original theme stories. In some of the collections each story explored a particular value and in the most recent (*Environmental Learning for Classroom and Assembly*) each story draws upon the magic of the natural world. In this present book, the power of story to promote learning has been intensified by focusing on adventure stories – the genre most immediately exciting and accessible to the primary school child.

Adventure stories are exciting because they involve risk and danger and have a hero who must be brave and resourceful in facing these dangers. This is the kind of hero with whom the children will enjoy identifying. Adventure stories are often quest stories, with the hero seeking to fulfil a mission (running to) or fleeing danger (running from). Sometimes they are transformational stories in which the journey is an inner one leading to the hero's transformation. Both types of story are provided.

Because these are exciting adventure stories they hook the child's interest. They also focus on child-friendly topics to lead into a range of learning activities – subject based, cross-curricular and interdisciplinary. These are presented and utilised to educate as they entertain.

Though the child-friendly topics have been chosen with boys in mind, we have not neglected the girls. Thus in Chapter 3 the boy hook is football but the story theme of bullying is of concern to both boys and girls. In Chapter 7 the planes, boats and trains are boy hooks, but Grace Darling is a female heroine. In

Chapters 6 and 8 the boy hook is cars (charismatic and racing cars respectively), but Chapter 8 has the story theme of friendship and Chapter 6 includes an additional, complementary story with girl appeal ('Prince Henry and the Wedding'). Chapters 1, 2, 4 and 5 have universal appeal – covering space travel, quests, terrorists and ghosts!

Learning across the curriculum

Adventures stories, illustrations and photocopiable resources are provided to stimulate a range of enjoyable activities for learning across the curriculum. The learning activities provided can be used with flexibility to suit key stages one and two.

Once again, following the Rose Report, there is an emphasis on cross-curricular learning. Therefore, in this book, the learning activities cover:

- Subject-centred work including all the subjects of the National Curriculum

- Cross-curricular values and cross-curricular thinking skills

- Interdisciplinary learning

What is meant by subject-centred work?

Subject-distinctive concepts, understanding and skills in each of the subjects of the National Curriculum (which themselves correspond to the distinctive forms of human knowledge). Over the eight chapters as a whole, learning activities for all areas of the National Curriculum are included.

What is meant by cross-curricular work?

Concepts, understanding and skills, such as cross-curricular values, cross-curricular critical thinking skills, cross-curricular creativity, which are generic, permeating all areas of the curriculum.

Perhaps the most important cross-curricular skills are those required for literacy development. We provide activities for literacy development in close association with each chapter's story. In most chapters we also provide activities for values education, activities to foster creativity and in Chapter 5 (to balance the supernatural theme of the story) practice in critical thinking.

What do we mean by interdisciplinary work?

Topics which readily lend themselves to work in several different areas of the curriculum, enabling staff to contribute to a common project from their different areas of expertise. Such readily interdisciplinary topics include the Olympics, transport, the universe, the environment and so on.

We have chosen a mixture of topics including the familiar (travel), the topical (the Olympics) and those of importance to society (the environment) and to the school (bullying).

This threefold classification of knowledge is useful. However, we must also recognise that these categories themselves overlap. For example, a critical questioning approach to any material is a generic cross-curricular thinking skill. However, it finds expression in different ways in the different domains and children will need to come to recognise these differences. Similarly, an interdisciplinary topic could draw on all subject areas and in this sense cross the curriculum, though time constraints usually mean that major contributions to a topic come from just three or four domains.

How to use the book

Eight original themed stories introduce eight chapters. As has been described above, the learning activities are divided into literacy development, the specific areas of the national curriculum, cross-curricular values and skills, and topics to encourage interdisciplinary learning.

Having introduced the theme of the story you can tell or read it, perhaps with the children sitting in a circle. Deal with difficult vocabulary in your usual way, which will sometimes means explaining words as you come to them and sometimes explaining them in advance of the story. You can select from or add to the suggested activities. You may also wish to use some of the values-related activity as preparation for an assembly. In Chapters 2 and 3, for an assembly on the environment and on bullying respectively, suggested poems and songs are given, taken from commonly used texts, but you will not find it difficult to find alternatives which are relevant to the theme. It is an educative task to encourage the children themselves to make this selection. If you wish you can use this suggested structure for assemblies based on the value themes in other chapters: self-confidence in Chapter 1, friendship in Chapter 8, inclusion/cultural diversity in Chapters 3 and 4 and courage in almost every chapter.

At the beginning of each chapter the adventure story is a useful stimulation for literacy hour. The subsequent activities and photocopiable resources provided will cover several subsequent teaching sessions. However, you should set a pace which suits you and your class. Since the intended age range (key stages one and two) covers a wide range (four to eleven years) you should use the material at the developmental level appropriate to your children. Pointers are given. For example, in the literacy development activities, sequencing practice is given for younger or less able children, creative writing for key stage two and advanced story work for more able, older children. We hope that you and your class will enjoy the stories and the associated activities, and enjoy, too, the wonderful, 'grown-up' illustrations.

1

We have a problem

An adventure in space

Topics and themes

The boy-friendly topic for this chapter is space travel and the universal theme is the development of self-confidence. The story is about a boy who is the first child in space. His self-confidence is restored when his brave actions save the mission. The resources provide space-travel related activities, including material about the Apollo moon landing missions.

Literacy development

Introduce the story vocabulary in your usual way.

Read the story yourself but vary subsequent readings – the children reading aloud in turn or reading to themselves.

Talking about the story and the literacy activities provided aim to develop oracy, reading skills and practice in writing a science fiction story.

Subject areas

Science, History, Religious Education

Cross-curricular values

Personal education, the development of self-confidence
Spiritual values

Creativity

Particularly combining art and creative writing in illustrating and writing science fiction stories

Interdisciplinary projects

A space-related research project using ICT

Suggested resources

Four photocopiable pages are provided

Books

Fiction

Real Life Pilot Stories – Going Solo, Roald Dahl (Penguin)
Astrazores – The Sun Snatchers, Steve Cole (Red Fox)

Non-fiction

Why is Snot Green?, Glen Murphy (Macmillan Children's Books)
Learning through Science, various authors (Macdonald Education)
The Best Book of the Moon, Ian Graham (Kingfisher)
Space Travel, M. Leicester and E. Garret (LCP Cross-curricular ebooks)

Web sites

www.guardian.co.uk/science
http://en.wikipedia.org/wiki/Apollo_13

Other

Obtain a bulk library loan on space travel.
If possible arrange a class visit to a science museum or to the space centre at Leicester.

Music

The Planets, Gustav Holst

Vocabulary

Congratulations	Happy praises
Thrilled	Excited and pleased
Dented	Made a hollow by hitting
Experienced	Having done something before
Envious	Jealous
Pipsqueak	Small like an orange pip
Ignore	Take no notice; give no attention
Taunts	Jeers
Strange	Odd
Determination	Resolve; having a steadfast decision
Cells	Part of a battery
Power	Use of energy
Hero	A brave person who is honoured for his bravery

Space travel-related vocabulary

Space	Beyond earth's atmosphere
Apollo	The name of several moon missions
Crew	The vehicle's staff members
Astronauts	Members of the crew of a spacecraft
Lunar	To do with the moon
Lunar module	Part of the spacecraft: the part that goes down to the moon
Launched	Take off from earth
Oxygen tanks	Containers for oxygen gas
Houston	Space station in Texas, USA

The story

We have a problem
An adventure in space

The children waited in complete silence for the Head Teacher to make his announcement. Pip, hearing his own full name, felt his heart lurch.

'Phillip Timms will join the Apollo flight team for the September moon mission. He will make history. The first child ever to go into space. Congratulations Phillip. We all wish you well.'

Pip was thrilled. Sadly, his happiness was soon dented. Billy Bassey, who was standing next to Pip, leaned forward and whispered, 'It's only you because of your Mum and Dad.'

Pip's Mum and Dad were experienced astronauts who would be on the flight too. *Was that really why he'd been chosen*, he wondered.

Over the next few months, as Pip trained for the flight, he found out how envious and resentful the rest of the Space School children felt. They became less friendly. They never mentioned the September moon mission except once, when Ryan Ford said, 'No way would they have chosen a small pipsqueak like you. My Mum says you've been chosen because of your Mum and Dad. It's not fair.'

After that the name stuck and everyone called Pip 'Pipsqueak'.

Pip asked his Dad if what Ryan had said was true.

'It's not only because of us, Pip. They wouldn't have chosen you if you weren't in tip top shape and very bright.'

Pip decided to ignore the taunts, though they still bothered him. He worked extra hard at his training. *I'll show everyone,* he thought.

The night before the flight, Pip was too excited to sleep. He tossed and turned. When he did sleep he had strange mixed-up dreams and a nightmare about failing to secure the basket of a hot air balloon. He and everyone in it hurtled towards the ground.

The next morning Pip and the crew entered the spacecraft. The crew members were pilot John Timms, Commander Marie Timms and lunar module pilot Fred Smith. They all smiled at Pip, whose cheeks felt sore from so much smiling. Somehow he couldn't stop his big broad grin.

FIGURE 1.1 We have a problem.

The crew did their various preparations whilst Pip watched, his excitement soaring like a rocket inside his chest. At last there was take-off. The mission successfully launched.

A few hours later, however, disaster struck. Pip heard a dull thud.

'There's an explosion in one of the service module's oxygen tanks,' his Dad said.

Pip saw that all the adults were looking very serious and he was afraid. Pip's Dad sent a radio message: 'Houston, we have a problem.'

'The command module will function on its own batteries,' Houston radioed back, but minutes later the lights began to dim, and Commander Marie Timms realised that the batteries were damaged.

'We need to get into the battery compartment to link out the damaged cells,' she said.

'The cable duct is too small,' said Fred Smith.

'Maybe I could get in,' said Pip.

Pip saw his Mother's face grow pale. 'I guess we have to let you try,' she said.

Pip felt a fierce determination. He had wanted to prove himself. This was his chance!

'You must breathe out, Pip, to squash into the cable duct,' said his Mum.

Pip took a deep breath and breathed out to make his chest go in, and pushed himself head first into the dark space. He had to take little breaths because of the force on his chest. He had to let out this air to push forward a few inches. It was scary and uncomfortable. He was frightened he might get stuck in there and die. Slowly, inch by inch, he moved through the tight duct. It took ten long minutes before he reached the batteries. He could hear his Mum's voice, a clear calm voice but Pip could hear the anxiety underneath.

'Look at the condition monitor at the end of each cell, Pip. If any show black instead of green you must unplug the two power plugs.'

Pip looked at each monitor in turn. There were four showing black. It was hard to unplug them. He used all the strength in his small fingers and managed, with difficulty, to unplug all eight. His mother was speaking again.

'Pip, after that, link up the good cells. Link up the good cells to make a battery. Like you did in the science class, Pip. Just like that.'

Pip looked very carefully to make sure he did it right. One wrong link would cause an explosion and kill them all. His hands were trembling as he made the final link. No explosion!

For a few moments Pip relaxed, but now came the most difficult task of all. Pip had to return down the narrow duct – backwards. Resisting the growing wish to take a deep deep breath he eased himself backwards, inch by slow inch. When at last he emerged into the space module he drew a huge breath and punched the air. The three astronauts clapped his back and his Dad gave him a high five. They were all speaking at once. 'Well done Pip. Brilliant. You've saved us.'

'An inch taller or fatter and you couldn't have got through that duct!' said Dad.

The team had to abandon the planned moon landing. Because the power was limited, the return to Earth was dangerous and very cold. Pip remained calm and brave. He felt a huge relief when splashdown was eventually achieved.

Back on Earth everyone had watched the mission's dramatic events on live TV. Pip's part in the safe return was known. He was the hero of the Apollo mission – a child hero. He had proved himself to the kids at the space school. He was their hero too. Almost better than this, though, was Pip's knowledge that he had, after all, been rightly chosen for the mission.

© Mal Leicester

Literacy development

Talking about the story

- What is Pip's full name?

- Why do the children at the Space School think Pip was chosen?

- Why did Pip go into the cable duct instead of one of the experienced astronauts?

- What did he have to do there?

- Back on Earth how did everyone know what Pip had done?

Points for discussion

- Discuss name calling as part of bullying behaviour. Why was Pipsqueak a mean name for Pip?

- Why was Pip much more self-confident by the end of the mission?

- Pip became a hero but he had been afraid. Do fear and bravery go together? (To be brave often involves overcoming your fear.)

Literacy activities

Science fiction stories combine science and imagination. Sometimes what the writer imagines turns out to be fact in the future. At one time space travel itself was science fiction and perhaps one day in the future aliens will become science fact.

Discuss with the children current science fiction television programmes such as *Doctor Who*. Consider showing a science fiction film or science fiction TV episode before the discussion. However much clothes or gadgets change, human nature and good and evil remain the same.

Give each child a copy of the story printed on the photocopiable pages at the end of the chapter. Simplify and tell the story to younger children in your usual way and use it for class reading with older children. In discussion with the children, compare 'We Have a Problem' with 'An Alien Friend' (e.g. similarities: both are science fiction, both are about a boy; differences: one happens in space and one on Earth, one has an alien and one does not).

KS1

The children make up and tell or draw or write their own space adventure story. They can create the story working as individuals, in pairs or in small groups.

KS2

The children write their own science fiction story involving the hero meeting an alien or aliens who may or may not be friendly. More gifted children could try to bring some real science into their story, just as there is real science about batteries in 'We Have a Problem' and about magnetism in 'An Alien Friend'.

Subject-based activities

Science

Batteries are made up from a number of cells. Each cell has a positive terminal and a negative terminal. Bring a used PP3 battery and show that it has a positive terminal and a negative terminal. Take the battery apart to show that it is made up from a number of cells connected together in series. (In the PP3 the cells will probably look like miniature slices of bread.) Cells come in different shapes and sizes. Some are long and thin, such as AAA cells. Some are quite fat, such as D cells. Show the children an AAA and a D cell. Although these are called batteries, in fact these are only single cells. Take the wrapping off one to prove your point. Explain that the positive terminal is at the end with the nipple in the middle and the negative terminal is at the flat end of the cell. Each cell is about one and a half volts of electricity, so to make a three-volt battery two cells are joined in series with the positive of one cell joined to the negative of the other. These types of cell are made so that if you put the nose to tail, in a torch for instance, they are automatically connected in series, positive to negative. The children will probably be familiar with putting individual cells, the right way round, into battery-powered toys to make them work.

Give each of the children a copy of the photocopiable page and ask them to draw in the wires to connect the cells in series to form a six-volt battery from the four one-and-a-half-volt cells (plus to minus on each adjacent cell). Then, ask them to draw in the wires to connect the battery to the light bulb.

The teacher should have prepared four cells, anything from size AAA up to size D, each cell with a 100 mm flying wire held onto each end with sticky tape to look like Figure 1.2 and have a six-volt torch bulb ready for the experiment. Show the class how you join up the cells to form a battery and then connect the battery to the bulb to show a bright light. You can reverse a cell to show that the light is much dimmer.

SAFETY NOTICE

Do not short the cells out as this may cause excessive heat in the wires or a cell to eject liquid or gas.

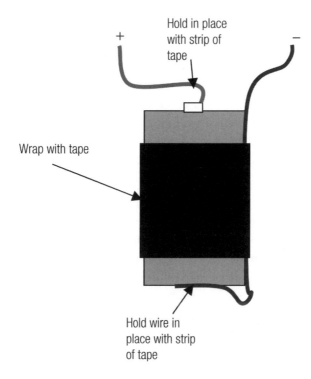

FIGURE 1.2 D cell as two-port cell.

Art

ILLUSTRATING SCIENCE FICTION STORIES

Show the children the illustration on the cover of the book and the story illustration. Discuss how these are different. (One coloured/one black and white; one straight-sided/one flowing; . . .). Talk about how illustrations differ. For example:

■ Type: abstract or semi-abstract or representational or a mixture

■ Colour: black and white or monochrome or two colours or full colour

■ Style: simple or complicated, dynamic or static etc.

■ Materials: ink, pencil, coloured pencils, crayons, paint

A good illustration must match well with the story it is illustrating. (A black and white picture might suit a gloomy story and a brightly coloured picture a happy one.) Ask the children to think up some other examples. Now ask the children to do an illustration for three different science fiction stories: 'We Have a Problem', 'An Alien Friend' and the story they wrote for themselves. They must try to make three very different choices (colour, style, type, materials).

Religious Education

Space travel, fact or fiction, is a good way into fundamental questions about the universe. How did it come into being? Must it have been created by God? Is there life on other planets and what is the meaning of human life? Learning about our amazing galaxy gives rise to the spiritual emotions of wonder and awe.

Maths

Photocopy the picture on the front cover of the book onto card, for each of the children. Cut card down to the size of the picture. Using black pen the children draw jigsaw shapes on the back of the card, cut these out and swap with classmates to enjoy doing jigsaws – a practice with shape and spatial awareness.

Cross-curricular values

Self-confidence

In pairs, the children work at developing a dialogue. The children decide on two characters. One of these characters lacks self-confidence. Perhaps they are shy or feel they are not good at anything. The other is a kind friend. Each pair decides who their characters are (e.g. their name, gender, age, occupation, personality). Each child pretends to be one of these characters. The aim is to have a conversation, with each child as one of the characters, in which the character with little self-confidence becomes more self-confident during the dialogue/conversation.

Older, more able children could try to develop the dialogue into a short play.

Interdisciplinary project

A space research project

Using the school IT suite and the bulk library loan, the children can undertake a space-related research project. Let the children select a topic of their choice. Here are some possibilities:

- Choose two of the planets in our solar system and write what we know about them – Mercury, Venus, Mars, Jupiter, Saturn, Uranus, Neptune (exclude the Earth)

- Telescopes (in general, or a particular telescope such as the Hubble telescope or the telescope at Jodrell Bank)

- Asteroids and/or meteors

- The atmosphere

- The Sun

The children should collect the information and write this into an information piece. Some of these could be read out to the class.

An alien friend

The ball landed at my feet. I stared down. It was the same make as my favourite one, which I had recently lost.

'Here mate!' someone yelled.

I looked over and saw a group of boys in the next field. They were all watching me expectantly. I picked up the ball. I wanted it, and without stopping to think, instead of chucking it back, I turned and ran, clutching it in my arms. I was at the edge of a wood, and fled into it.

I could hear angry yells behind. Scared, I ran as fast as I could, hardly aware of the stinging nettles at my ankle or the sharp thorns pulling at my clothes. The boys were catching me up.

I was often in the wood and headed for a big old tree with a thin hollow in its side. I knew I could squeeze in there and that it was easy to miss. I had to hold the ball at my side and breathe in as I edged through. My heart was thudding and my breath coming in gulps. Surely they would hear me. I could hear them, very close, and one of the boys yelled to the others.

'We've lost him. He'll be out of the wood and across one of the fields. Come on lads, I'm off.'

I heard him tramp back the way we had run. Other voices reached my ears, and I could tell that the rest of the gang were following him back. When they had all gone and silence returned I felt my body relax, but now my mind was churning, full of guilt like dirty water in Mum's washing machine. I'd stolen their ball! I was a thief! I felt sick. And the worst of it was, I didn't know the boys so I couldn't give it back.

My eyes had got used to the darkness inside my tree and I noticed a shelf in front of me. Only it wasn't a shelf because it wasn't attached to the tree. It wasn't resting on anything – nor was it suspended from above like a swing. I passed my hand above and below and around it. It was just hanging there. In the air. There were two peculiarly shaped bottles on the shelf. Like the shelf itself, they were hanging in the air, about one centimetre above it.

'I could help you give it back,' said a voice from above me.

I felt my mouth drop open as I looked up, too amazed to be frightened. The voice came in waves, like lightly pattering rain.

'I won't harm you.'

'Who are you? Where are you?'

'I'm from the planet Japonica. I came up here so I wouldn't frighten you. I look different from you, you see'.

'Different. How?' I asked, feeling uneasy now. Had a mad person climbed up inside the tree – or was he really an alien? Or was I dreaming?

'I have several arms, well, more like the trunks of Earth elephants, and eyes all around my head. Eleven.'

'Eleven eyes!'

'And I'm a sort of indigo colour.'

'Why are you here?'

'In the tree or on your Earth?'

'Ehrr . . . both.'

'On Earth to investigate how electromagnetic forces work here. By the way, I've used those forces to suspend the shelf and the bottles up here, and me, come to that. And we use the same forces to bend space when we travel to other planets. For the tiniest fraction of time we can bring another planet close enough to reach it.'

'Wow!' I said. 'Like folding paper to make two dots touch.'

'Exactly! I'm in the tree to keep away from humans. You're quite an aggressive species you know, which is really very sad. Shall I come down now? Ready?'

'Y . . . yes,' I said.

And there he was, small enough to stand on the shelf in front of me. His bluish skin sort of glowed. I have to admit, his ring of green eyes was scary, but his mouth curved up, like a dolphin's, which made him look friendly.

'I'm Jofod,' he said.

'I'm Max.'

'Max, I could use magnetic forces to float that ball. It could follow in the wake of one of those boys. I could have it come to rest in his garden. Do you want me to?'

'Oh, yes please, Jofod,' I said.

I felt myself go hot with shame.

'It doesn't belong to me, you see'.

'Let go,' said Jofod, 'of the ball and of your guilt.'

I opened my arms and the ball hovered in the air before floating out of the opening in the tree. I watched it float away, over the trees, back, I was sure, to its owner. I felt such a sweet relief, as though my guilt really had floated away with the ball.

Adventure Stories for Reading, Learning and Literacy, Routledge © Mal Leicester and Roger Twelvetrees, 2010

'Thank you,' I whispered.

'Would you do me a favour in return?' Jofod asked.

I really wanted to, but I couldn't imagine how I could help someone who could do the things that Jofod could. I didn't know what to say.

'Max, I simply want you not to tell anyone about me for one full hour after you leave here. OK?'

'That's all? Of course I won't.'

'Thanks Max. It won't be as easy as you think.' Jofod's light voice seemed to have a smile in it.

I looked at my watch. It was four o'clock already. I had to go home then, but I was sorry to leave.

'Bye, Jofod, and thanks,' I said.

He touched my arm gently with one of his trunks.

'Goodbye, Max, and thanks to you too.'

It was half past four when I got to my house. Mum gave me a glass of milk and some biscuits and sat with me in the kitchen to chat. I was dying to tell her about Jofod. I watched the big kitchen clock. It would need to be five o'clock before I would have left Jofod for one full hour. That remaining half hour crawled by but at last it was five o'clock and I told Mum about Jofod. She laughed!

'You've got a great imagination Max,' she said. 'That was almost too real.'

I tried to convince her. I even confessed about stealing the ball and Mum looked worried until I got to the part about Jofod floating it back to the boys. Then she smiled, taking it all for make-believe.

'You must write down your story,' she said.

The next day it was sunny and I asked Mum to come for a walk and feeling very excited I took her and my little sister into the wood as far as my tree. I was longing for them to meet my new friend. As we approached the tree, I suddenly realised what we would find. Jofod and all trace of him had gone! He had returned to Japonica. I felt sad and hoped that one day he would come back to see me. I knew that I would never forget my alien friend.

© Mal Leicester

We are grateful to LCP for allowing us to reproduce this story, which is taken from the efile 'Space Travel', which is part of their Cross-curricular Files.

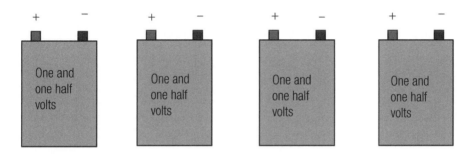

FIGURE 1.3 Diagram of a battery.

2

The Long Swim

A river adventure

Topics and themes

The boy-friendly topic for this chapter is a dangerous journey and the universal themes are coming of age and migration. The story is about a brave water-zeddar (an imaginary creature) who must leave home to make the Long Swim to find a new home and a wife. The resources provide environmental-related activities and classroom resources.

Literacy development

Introduce the story vocabulary in your usual way.

Read the story yourself but vary subsequent readings – the children reading aloud in turn or reading to themselves.

Talking about the story and the literacy activities provided aim to develop oracy, reading skills and practice in a variety of writing forms.

Subject areas

Geography, Physical Education (swimming), Science (natural history), Music/Science

Cross-curricular values

Cultural values – migration

Creativity

Particularly combining science with music and with creative writing in the subject-based activities

Interdisciplinary projects

Environmental education
Environmental assembly

Suggested resources

Four photocopiable pages are provided

Books

Fiction

The Lorax (new edn 1997), Dr Seuss (Picture Lions)
Oi! Get Off My Train, J. Burningham (Red Fox)
Ring of Bright Water, G. Maxwell (Penguin Books)
Tarka the Otter, H. Williamson (Puffin Classics)

Non-fiction

Hands-on Nature: Information and Activities for Exploring the Environment with Children, J. Lingelbach *et al.* (University Press of New England)
Language Arts and Environmental Awarenesss: 100+ Integrated Books and Activities for Children, P. Roberts (Shoestring Press)
Discovering Marine Mammals: A Nature Activity Book, N. Field and S. Machlis (Dog-Eared Publications)

Web sites

BBC – Natural History: www.bbc.co.uk/sn
Eden Project: www.edenproject.com
Natural History Museum: www.nhm.ac.uk
Wildlife Trusts: www.wildlifetrusts.org.uk

Other

There are many videos, DVD and television documentaries about the natural world. There are also many films on the public broadcast service (PBS) website at www.pbs.org/wnet/nature.

Vocabulary

Water-zeddar	An imaginary creature a bit like an otter
Journeyed	Travelled
Adventurous	Full of daring events
Brave	Showing courage
Farewell	Goodbye
Advice	Counsel, suggestions meant to be helpful
Forest	Big wood, large area of trees
Hounds	Hunting dogs
Pike	A particular fish – one which has sharp teeth
Bordering	On the edge of
Baying	Barking, like a large dog
Ferocious	Fierce
Gleam	Shine
Triumphant	Successful, victorious

The story

The Long Swim

'The time has come for you to make the Long Swim,' said Lona, Alpha's mother. 'You have grown to be a fine, strong water-zeddar.'

Alpha looked down into his mother's face and saw pride and sadness in her eyes.

'You must find a wife and raise a family of your own,' she told him.

Alpha didn't want to leave his mother and father, or his brothers and sisters or their warm den by the lake. He remembered his father's stories about the olden days, before Alpha was even born; stories about the time long ago when Omega, his father, was young and had lived with his own mother. His father's mother had died and his father had made the Long Swim not knowing if he was the only water-zeddar left in the world. Omega had journeyed many adventurous miles before finding Lona and her lake. His father had been brave and heroic. Alpha felt anxious and scared. Could he be as brave as his father had been? Could he even reach the river and then make the Long Swim? Could he find a wife and be a strong father to their zeddies? He felt too frightened to try. *Not today!* he thought.

'I'll go tomorrow,' Alpha said.

The next day all his family gathered to say farewell to Alpha and his father gave him some advice.

'The stream from the lake to the river dried up long ago. To make your Long Swim you must first trek through the forest where the hounds sometimes hunt. Remember, if you hear them climb into a tree and hide.'

Alpha shivered. He was not good at climbing trees. Would one of these monsters catch him and tear him to pieces before he could reach the river? He was too frightened to set out.

'I'll go tomorrow,' he said. 'I'll have one more day with you.'

The next day all his family gathered again to say farewell to Alpha and once again his father gave some advice.

'Remember, in the river watch out for pike the whole time and swim for your life if a large one comes your way.'

'I'll go tomorrow,' Alpha said. 'I must say goodbye to all my friends.'

FIGURE 2.1 Water-zeddar.

The next day for the third time Alpha's family gathered together to see him off.

'Don't worry son, I know you can do it,' his father said.

Alpha touched noses with his mother and father and desperately wanting to be brave he took a deep breath and plunged into the thick and thorny forest bordering the lake.

For hours Alpha pushed his way through the dense undergrowth. He hated being so far from any water. His fur felt hot and itchy and his heart beat painfully in his chest. It seemed to stop altogether when in the distance he heard the baying of the hounds. Alpha remembered his father's advice and began to climb the nearest tree, digging in his claws for purchase and slowly heaving himself up. His progress was slow and the hounds sounded nearer. He reached the first branch and inched along. He hid in the leaves as a hound and its handler came into view. It sniffed round the base of the tree and looking up began to bark. Alpha peered down through the leaves and saw with horror the slavering jaws of the ferocious beast filled with rows of jagged teeth.

A chorus of barks was coming from the rest of the pack some way to one side of the tree and the handler was straining to pull the hound towards the sound.

'This way,' he commanded. 'Now I say!'

Reluctantly, still straining to look back, the hound was forced to follow.

Alpha stayed in the tree the rest of the day and through the long night. He couldn't sleep. His heart lurched at the hoot of an owl. Frozen with cold and with fright he listened to the noises from the dark. At last dawn crept over the forest and Alpha climbed down the tree. He hurried on, tired and hungry and longing for water both to plunge into and to drink.

Eventually he pushed past the final trees and to his delight gazed upon the river. It was wide and inviting and gleaming in the sun. Alpha plunged in and for a few joyous moments drank and splashed and dived in the wet welcoming water until out of the corner of his eye he caught a flash of the enemy – a huge pike was almost upon him.

Alpha swam as fast as he could, faster than he ever had before, faster and faster. The pike was snapping at his tail now. Alpha made a huge effort and with a final burst of speed managed to pull ahead just enough to twist towards the bank and clamber out gasping for air.

Alpha caught his breath but he had lost his nerve. He knew in his bones that he had not come far enough to complete the Long Swim, but he was too frightened to dive back into the water. Time passed and eventually, his father's words echoing in his mind – *you can do it, son* – Alpha dived back in and swam straight on as fast as he could, looking out for pike as he did so.

Later, as the sun began to set, he heard a change in the sound of the river. He could hear the sound of a huge fall of water ahead. He took a deep breath and as he came to the falls he dived with the water. He was flying with the water and when he hit the river far below he dived deep deep down before curving up and leaping out through the water's surface into the bright air. He shook diamond droplets from his whiskers and somehow his fear shook away too.

Some miles further on Alpha came into quieter waters. He had left the forest behind. There were green fields on each side and on his right the gleam of a lake. Alpha headed towards it. When he arrived it felt like the proper end of the Long Swim.

Out of the water rose a female water-zeddar. She was beautiful and she was smiling at him, a dolphin-like smile. Her fur was reddish brown and her eyes were as bright as the water. Alpha snatched a silver fish from the lake and held it out to her. They feasted on it together. Alpha felt happy, triumphant and at home.

Alpha and Aquilane lived together in a dry den under one of the lakeside trees. The den was similar to the home Alpha had grown up in and had left behind. Tree roots like glimmering ivory appeared and disappeared in the mud floor and the walls and rounded ceiling were made of wood. Alpha and Aquilane were happy in the hidden den, and one wonderful day Aquilane had a beautiful tiny zeddie. They gazed in delight at his pointed nose and his soft, brown fur.

'His name shall be Omega,' Alpha said.

© Mal Leicester

Literacy development

Talking about the story

- What relation to you is your father's mother?

- How can we tell that Alpha did not want to go on his Long Swim?

- What three scary things happened on his journey?

- Who did he meet at the end?

Points for discussion

- Why was it time for Alpha's Long Swim?

- Was Alpha brave? (Give reasons for your answer.)

- Give some reasons why young adult humans leave home.

Literacy activities

KS1

For less able and young children give photocopiable page 29. Read the story once more and the children must write 1 or 2 or 3 on each picture in the correct order in which they occur in the story. (They are not in the correct order on the page.)

KS2

Use the photocopiable story 'Morris and the Scrill' as a class read. Talk about how Morris was kind to the blackbird and ways in which we can be kind to birds and other creatures. The children write their own story about a creature (real like the blackbird, or imaginary like the water-zeddar) with some children able to match the creature and its environment (habitat, food, etc.).

Point of view

For gifted and older children use the story to explore point of view. 'The Long Swim' is told from Alpha's viewpoint and so we don't mind him eating the silver fish and we want him to escape from the pike. A story from the pike's point of view would make us anxious for the hungry pike to catch a meal! The children could write the meeting between Alpha and Aquilane from Aquilane's point of view.

The Olympics and Paralympics

Remind the children of Alpha's skills in the story. He had to climb quickly up trees. He had to swim faster than the pike. He had to swim really well and gracefully over the waterfall. These are the kinds of abilities that our athletes develop. Think of the top athletes competing in various events in the Olympics and Paralympics. You could talk with the children about the Olympics and the coming Olympics in London. Perhaps some of the children would like to do some research on either the Olympics or the Paralympics and choose one of the top athletes who won medals at the last Olympics. They should draw (KS1) or write a piece about (KS2) their athlete of choice.

Subject-centred activities

Geography

Mapping the blue planet

Photocopy a world map from a school atlas. Give a copy to each of the children. They can see for themselves how much of the Earth is ocean. They can also see how the main continents would once have almost fitted together like a giant jigsaw. In the 1960s this led scientists to accept the theory of plate tectonics.

Geologists agree that the Earth's surface is made up of about twelve major 'plates'. These solid plates ride on a sea of molten lava – sometimes pulling further apart and sometimes moving nearer together, sliding past each other or sometimes colliding.

These movements create oceans, mountains, earthquakes, volcanoes and islands. The Earth is thus constantly changing.

Let the children cut out the continents and place them together like an inexact jigsaw.

Now the children should cooperate together on making a big class map for the classroom wall.

Physical Education/Sport Education

At the children's next swimming lesson they could take turns to be the pike and then Alpha, with the pike trying to catch up with Alpha (the teacher will set the start given to Alpha according to the relative ability of the children). They can also practise diving as though they were going over a waterfall.

Science (natural history)

Water and plants

Plants need water to stay alive and to grow. Most plants take in water through their roots. It goes up tiny 'pipes' (capillaries) to the plant's leaves and flowers.

Drop red food dye in a glass of water. Add some flowers to the glass of water. The flowers will 'drink' the water (i.e. the water is taken up the stem to the blossom); within an hour the children will see the flower changing colour. The coloured water has reached the blossom!

Some desert plants such as cacti can store water and provide a life-saving drink for people who know the right plants!

Water and rain

The sun warms up the water in the sea. This turns into a gas (water vapour). Wind carries the water vapour up into the sky where the air is cooler and turns the vapour into tiny water droplets. These droplets join together to make a cloud and over high ground, where the air gets even cooler, they grow so heavy that they fall to the Earth as rain.

Let the children pretend to be a drop of water. They draw or write a story from when the drop rises from the sea as water vapour until it falls back to Earth as rain. How the drop of water feels, what it sees and where it lands are for the child to decide. Alternatively they could write a poem called 'The Rain Drop'.

Music and Science

Gaia

James Lovelock believed that we must think of the world as an interdependent mix of systems and cycles and he called this totality of interaction Gaia. Richard Fortey (President of the Geological Society) likens this to Bach's *B Minor Mass* with its interwoven melodic threads. You could play this as part of the natural science activities.

One wonderful example of interdependence is photosynthesis: the process whereby trees and green plants take in carbon dioxide and exude the oxygen we need. We breathe in the oxygen and exhale carbon dioxide.

What other interdependencies can the children suggest? (Example: bees scattering pollen.)

Cross-curricular values

Cultural values – migration

As part of a multicultural, inclusive education the children should learn about migration and immigration. One strong form of social prejudice is directed against 'immigrants'. The children should understand the facts (in history, in geography etc.) and develop more positive, empathetic attitudes (literature, personal experience, multicultural arts, cuisines, costumes, customs etc.).

The chapter story ('The Long Swim') sees the migration of the water-zeddar in search of a new home and wife. Thus science (natural history) makes a positive contribution to our understanding of human migration – which is also often instigated for economic and family reasons. Following 'Morris and the Scrill' you could also talk about the migration of birds and the birds, such as blackbirds, which remain here for the winter.

Ask if any of the children have moved home. Where did they move from and where did they move to? Why did the family move home? Let the children talk about the experience of moving.

You could use the map previously made by the children to show longer migrations, for example where some British children's parents and grandparents came from (for example India, the Caribbean, Africa) and where recent European immigrants are travelling from. In a multicultural school the children could perhaps do recorded interviews with family members who actually migrated to Britain and who could share their experiences. Perhaps the children could choose one of these places for a class project as part of their Geography lessons.

Interdisciplinary activities

Environmental Education

In *Environmental Learning for Classroom and Assembly* (M. Leicester and D. Taylor, Fulton/Routledge 2009), the learning activities are divided into appreciation of nature; conservation; and protection and enhancement. Here are some suggested activities using these categories which fit in with the story 'The Long Swim'.

Appreciation: a nature walk

Take the children on a walk through the school grounds to collect objects for a nature display (grasses, leaves, tree bark, twigs, conkers, fir cones, stones, daisies etc.).

If it is feasible, older children could be taken on a canal or riverside walk and note all the creatures they see (fish, ducks, horses, cows, sheep, dogs, dragonflies, birds etc.).

Conservation: recycle your rubbish

The children bring in old boxes, cardboard rolls, plastic bottles, fabric, string etc., old birthday and Christmas cards or postcards, and broken games and toys.
Provide glue, paint and safe scissors.

- Let the children make their own imaginary creature using the 'rubbish'.

- Brainstorm with the children some gifts they could make, for example treasure box, bookmark, framed picture, classroom or bedroom mobile, cardboard sculpture, face mask. Let each child make a gift.

Protection and enhancement: litter hunt

Have a discussion with the children about why dropping litter is bad. (It can hurt small creatures, like the water-zeddar, it looks untidy, it causes accidents, it can spread disease etc.)

The children collect litter from the playground and fields. Back in the classroom they can draw a map showing where their litter was found.

NB: The Leicester and Taylor book contains many more such environmental education activities. It also contains the prequel to 'The Long Swim'. The story of Omega's adventurous journey is told ('The Last Water-Zeddar') as well as an extinction story about a butterfly ('Fragments of Fallen Sky').

Environmental assembly

The environment theme would be a good choice for a school assembly and would bring in creative writing, music and song, moral and spiritual values.

Photocopiable page 32 provides a fully planned assembly on this theme.

The children can practise and use this assembly and/or use this as a model to construct an assembly using stories, poems and prayers written by the children and incorporating their own choice of an appropriate hymn or song.

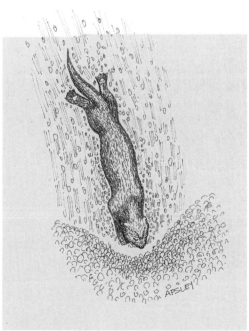

Morris and the scrill

An extract from Book Three of the Cosy Park Series

(Morris has heard an alarming noise coming from his engine and thinks it means his engine is broken.)

By the time they drove into Cosy Park Garage Morris was very frightened.

'What's the matter?' said Mr Fettler. 'Do you feel poorly? Open your bonnet for me please, wide as you can.'

Morris opened his bonnet and, fluttering and scrilling loudly, out flew a blackbird, straight over Mr Fettler's shoulder, just missing his nose. It made him jump in surprise, and young Bubble tried not to giggle. The blackbird flew round and round, high in the garage.

'Scrill-scrill-scrill,' came the same alarming whistle that Morris had heard before.

He was amazed. 'There's that engine noise again, but my engine's stopped,' he said. 'How can it whistle?'

'It wasn't your engine. It was that blackbird's alarm call,' said Percy (who knew about birdsongs).

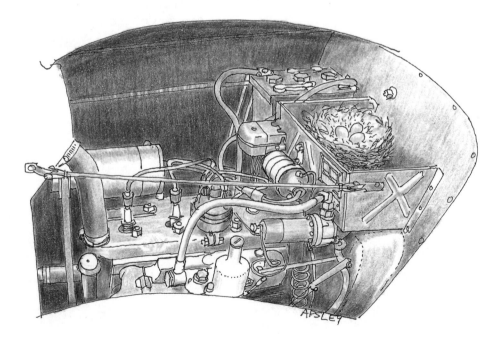

FIGURE 2.4 Morris with Blackbird.

'And just look, the blackbird has built her nest in the toolbox behind your engine, Morris, and laid three eggs,' said Mr Fettler.

'Was that scrill really a bird?' Morris exclaimed, hardly daring to hope.

Mr Fettler nodded.

'Well it wasn't your engine that just flew out was it?' joked Bubble.

All the cars laughed. Even Mr Fettler chuckled, but, just to be sure, he climbed under Morris to check for oil leaks, and the blackbird flew down to check on her eggs.

'Don't look so worried, Morris,' he said. 'You're fine.'

Morris smiled from headlight to headlight.

'Leave your bonnet open until the eggs are hatched and the little birds are big enough to fly away,' said Mr Fettler.

For several long weeks Morris missed his daily outings but, at last, one wonderful day, the eggs cracked and the tiny chicks pushed through.

'Cheep, cheep,' they said.

'Don't let any cats near my baby blackbirds, Dog,' Morris said, anxiously.

'Woof woof,' agreed Dog.

Dog and Morris continued to look after the blackbirds until one day the mother blackbird said, ' It's time for me to go now, but thank you Morris and thank you Dog.'

She flew out of Cosy Park Garage leading her new family behind her.

Mr Fettler removed the nest and set it on a high shelf just inside the big doors.

'Next year she can nest there instead of inside your tool box, Morris.'

At last Morris was able to close his bonnet again. The hinge was stiff and his whole body ached. Mr Fettler gently washed his paintwork clean.

'You've been very patient, Morris. It's too late today, but tomorrow you can go and see Bouncer again. Your engine is fine.'

© Mal Leicester and Roger Twelvetrees

An assembly structure

1 Theme: the environment

The teacher or one of the children introduces the assembly theme. Example: today we are thinking about our environment – in our home, in our school and across the whole world. How can we protect and enhance our environment and help to protect the fragile Earth?

2 A story

A child reads 'The Last Water-Zeddar'
or
Two or three children read out their own Rain Drop story.

3 A song

The children choose an appropriate song. For example, 'The World Is Such a Lovely Place'.

4 A prayer or (for a universal, humanistic or multifaith assembly) a quiet reflection

The children could write their own prayer or quiet reflection. Examples:

Prayer

Almighty God, thank you for creating our beautiful and wonderful earth – for the seas, mountains, rain and rain drops; for the flowers, trees and plants; for the wild creatures such as lions, elephants and polar bears. Help us to appreciate and look after our planet.

Amen.

Quiet reflection

Close your eyes and think of all the wonderful things on this earth. (Pause.) Let us be thankful for the oceans, mountains, the beautiful flora and wonderful fauna. (Pause.) Let us resolve to protect our planet. (Pause.) Think of one thing that you could do today for your environment. (Pause.)

3

The beautiful game

Topics and themes

The boy-friendly topic for this chapter is football and the universal theme is the prevention of bullying. The story is about a boy who is bullied at school until he becomes a school football hero. The resources provide football-related activities, classroom games that are both educative and fun, and anti-bullying learning materials.

Literacy development

Introduce the story vocabulary in your usual way.

Read the story yourself but vary subsequent readings – the children reading aloud in turn or reading to themselves.

Talking about the story and the literacy activities provided aim to develop oracy, reading skills and practice in a variety of writing forms.

Subject areas

Physical Education (including Sport Education and Dance), Maths

Cross-curricular values

Anti-bullying (i.e. respect, empathy, kindness)
Cooperation
Self-esteem

Creativity

Particularly combining movement, music and imagination in the work on dance above

Interdisciplinary projects

Constructing an anti-bullying school assembly
Constructing and playing board games for the classroom

Suggested resources

Four photocopiable pages are provided

Books

Fiction

Horrid Henry and the Football Fiend, F. Simon and A. Ross (Puffin)
Stories for Inclusive Schools, M. Leicester and G. Johnson (Routledge Falmer)

Non-fiction

Literacy in Action: Football, 24 Flexible Lessons for Ages 9–11, H. Butler (Routledge)
The Really Useful Physical Education Book, G. Stidder and S. Hayes (Eds) (Routledge)
Child Welfare in Football, An Exploration of Children's Welfare in the Modern Game, C. Brackenridge, A. Pitchford, K. Russell and G. Nutt (Routledge)
No More Stinking Thinking. A Work Book For Teaching Children Positive Thinking, J. Altiero (Jessica Kingsley)
Tackling Bullying in Schools, D. Guiney (Continuum Group)

Web sites

Several professional football clubs have community programmes for schools in their area, for example:

■ Birmingham City Football in the Community: www.footballfoundation.org. uk/our-schemes/premier-league-pfa-community-fund/birmingham-city-football-in-the-community/?locale=en

The aim of the department is to improve the quality of life within the community through football, regardless of social status, ethnic origin, gender, location or level of ability.

- Stoke City Football Club Community Programme: www.footballfoundation. org.uk/our-schemes/premier-league-pfa-community-fund/stoke-city-football-club-community-programme/?locale=en

Stoke City Football Club's community programme reaches out to over 350 schools in the surrounding area, aiming to help young people strive for an improved lifestyle with the help of sport.

Also there are sites that offer help and advice to anyone intending to give football coaching:

- Youth soccer coaching advice, drills, practice, plans etc.: www.footy4kids. co.uk/

- Football Association Safeguarding Children Best Practice:
www.thefa.com/TheFA/WhatWeDo/FootballSafe/~/media/Files/
PDF/TheFA/ClubAnnualMembershipInfoConsentForm.ashx/
ClubAnnualMembershipInfoConsentForm.pdf

Vocabulary

To worry	To be anxious, to fear something bad may happen
Strange	Odd
Ashamed	Felt bad as though he had done something wrong
Cheerfully	Happily
Sharp lookout	Look carefully for someone coming
Miserable	Sad
Anxious	Worried
Scared	Frightened
Gel	Set (like a jelly does)

More advanced vocabulary

Chief tormentors	Those being most cruel
Serve you right	A saying that means you deserve it
Chanting	Rhythmic shouting
Shin	Bone between knee and ankle
Coward	Someone who is the opposite of brave
Slunk off	Walked slowly away with heads down
Swabbing	Dabbing (at a bleeding cut)
Ignored	Taken no notice of, given no attention
Modestly	Not showing off

Opinion	What you think; your point of view
Realised	Understood
Accurately	Correctly

Football-related vocabulary

Trials	Tests for team selection
To coach	To show someone how to play a sport better
Practice	Doing something again and again to get better at it
Athletic	Fit and strong
Skill	Ability
Pass	Kick the ball to another member of the team
Dribble	Move the ball keeping it near your boots and without losing it to an opposing player
Control	Mastery of the ball
Left midfield	The position between the centre forward and the left wing player
Beautiful game	A well-known name for football
Football final	The last game in a knockout series
Footie	Slang for football
Team	The eleven players who play together as one side in a football game
Tactics	Team plans or tricks to gain an advantage over the other opposing team

The story

The beautiful game

Scott hated his new school. From the start the school bullies picked on him. One morning he nearly told his Mum, but he didn't want to worry her and for some strange reason he almost felt ashamed. In any case, she was rushing about not wanting to be late for work. Instead he said goodbye as cheerfully as he could and, as usual, bravely set out by himself. He kept a sharp lookout for any of his chief tormentors. Turning the final corner he saw four of them.

'Hey you, potty Scotty,' one shouted, and all four began to run towards him.

Scott darted back the way he had come. He tripped and fell, scraping his knee. The four bullies gathered round him laughing.

'Serve you right,' one said, 'bleed to death and die.'

The others joined in chanting, 'Die, die, die.'

Scott started to get up but was pushed back down. He was kicked hard on his shin. It really hurt. He was frightened and covered his face.

'Hey you lot,' a man shouted from his garden. 'Cowards! Leave him alone!'

The four bullies slunk off. Scott stood up swabbing his knee.

'You OK lad?' asked the man.

'Yeah, thanks. Thanks very much.'

No one did anything to Scott at playtime but no one spoke to him either. He stood alone and ignored, feeling miserable and worrying about what might happen on the way home. Nothing did happen, but right up until the last day of term Scott was anxious and scared.

On the last day, just before home time Scott's teacher made an announcement to his class.

'Two members of the school football team are leaving today,' she said. 'We will need two new players in September and trials will be held the day before we start back. Anyone interested should come to the playing field on Wednesday 1st September at two o'clock.'

This gave Scott an idea. *No one ever bullies the kids on the school team*, he thought. That evening at teatime he said, 'Dad, you're really good at footie, aren't you?'

FIGURE 3.1 Goal!

'Not bad,' said Dad modestly, but with a huge grin.

'I was thinking,' said Scott, 'if you coach me and I really practise maybe I could make the school team.'

'Ye . . . es,' said Dad thoughtfully. 'You could be good if you practised enough. You're quite athletic. You've just not been interested before. Like the rest of your school work really, Scott.'

Scott worked hard that summer. Every day under Dad's coaching, he practised his football – practised and practised. He had never worked so hard at anything and gradually, as his skills increased, he realised he was enjoying himself. He learned how to pass, how to dribble, how to control the ball.

'You're in with a chance,' Dad said, 'especially with being left-footed you could play on the left.'

On 1st September Scott went to the school playing field. His heart sank when he saw that twelve kids had turned up for two places. During the trials Scott saw that at least two of the other boys were playing well and one of them even scored a goal. *That's it*, thought Scott, *I've had it*. He could hardly believe it when at the end the PE teacher pointed at him.

'You. Scott isn't it? You'll play left midfield. Miss any practice and you're out.'

Scott nodded. He was thrilled.

'I won't, sir,' he promised.

Once it was known he was in the school team, as Scott had hoped, the bullying stopped. Most lunchtimes he had football practice, and the other boys in the team, although they knew each other better, were always friendly.

As they practised together they seemed to gel as a team. Coming to know each other's game they sometimes seemed to think together and played at their best.

'You're beginning to understand tactics,' their teacher said.

And when the team got it right, play was simple and felt good and was beautiful to watch.

Just before half term the team were in the City Schools Football Final. The whole school turned out to watch, and Mums and Dads were there, including his own.

Scott was keyed up with excitement. His team played as hard as they could. Even so, with five minutes to go they were one-all with the other team. And then he had his chance. Boris passed to him and he saw a long shot ahead. He focussed on the goal posts. The crowd faded away. He fired the ball as hard and accurately as he could, to one side of their goalie, and his ball shot home. The whole crowd roared with excitement and his team mates crowded round him. He felt their friendly slaps on the back and heard a jumble of wonderful words. *Well done mate. Cheers. Scott. Cool.* The captain gave him a high five. *No wonder Dad calls football the beautiful game*, he thought.

It was not long after that glorious final that Scott realised that he was happy at school. He was no longer bullied and had found some good friends. He never forgot what it was like to be bullied, though, and he never stood by when he saw it. In this way he helped the whole school to change.

'And in my opinion,' his Mum said, 'that makes you even more of a hero than your football does.'

© Mal Leicester

Literacy development

Talking about the story

- Why did Scott hate his new school?

- Why did Scott feel miserable in the playground?

- How many new players did the team need?

- How did Scott become much better at football?

- Why was Scott happy in the end?

- Do you like stories with a happy ending?

- (Ask the children to talk about some stories/books which they like)

Points for discussion

- Why do you think Scott was picked on at his new school?

- Why didn't he tell his Mum?

- What should you do if you are bullied?

- 'Serve you right,' the bully said, but was that true?

- Why did the man in the garden describe the bullies as cowards?

- Was Scott's Dad good at football? (How do we know?)

- Why was it good that Scott was left-footed?

- Why did Scott's Mum say that Scott was a hero?

Literacy activities

KS1

Give each child a copy of photocopiable page 45. Each child can decide on the colours for Scott's strip – his shirt, shorts, socks and boots. The children carefully colour Scott's clothing in their chosen colours. They must try to keep within the line of the illustration. Take the opportunity to explain what happens if the ball goes over the line around the pitch.

When the children have completed their colouring ask them why they chose those colours. For example, the team supported by Dad might have red shirts, or blue might be the child's favourite colour, or yellow will contrast well with Dad's black clothes in the illustration.

The illustration if scaled down and copied onto the right hand half of an A4 piece of paper in landscape format could form the basis for the children's Father's Day cards or for a birthday card for a brother or friend.

KS2

Older children will enjoy writing their own sport story. This could of course be about football or the children could choose an alternative sporting activity, including horse jumping, netball, swimming etc.

Remind the children that a story should have a beginning, a middle and an end.

Beginning (the setup) – Scott is bullied
  Scott decides to try for the school football team (II)

Middle (the developments) – Scott practises with his Dad
  Scott attends the trials
  Scott is chosen for the team
  Scott practises with the team

End (resolution) – Scott scores the winning goal (C)
  Scott is no longer bullied
  Scott has some good friends

For gifted or enthusiastic children

Explain that the sentence marked II above is the inciting incident. This is what Scott (the hero) does which makes the developments happen. The sentence marked C above is the climax of the story which leads into the resolution/conclusion.

This is a transformational story in which the hero goes on an emotional journey through which he changes by the end. (Scott changes from victim to hero. He is no longer bullied and he stops the bullying of others. He is no longer miserable and friendless but is happy and has friends.)

Can the more able children create a story in which sport is used to solve the hero's problem and in which by the end the hero has changed in some way?

Subject-centred activities

Physical Education/Sport Education

In a PE lesson following the story the children may be motivated to improve their own skills of ball control.

In playing football they may become more conscious of team cooperation and tactics.

Dance

Use an appropriate piece of music (for example Ravel's *Bolero*). Work with the children to choreograph a dance based on a variety of activities with an imaginary ball. The climax for the music works well with scoring a goal.

If you can readily obtain a DVD of Torvill and Dean's ice dance to Ravel's *Bolero* this could be shown to the children.

Numeracy

Use photocopiable page 46 (football results) to do some number work with the children.

If this works well, in a subsequent teaching session you could use actual football results taken from that week's newspapers.

For example, for simple number recognition, how many goals did Chelsea FC score? For simple subtraction, by how many goals did each winning team win? For addition, how many winning goals were there in total?

For older children, what was the total number of goals scored by the home teams, and what was the total number of goals scored by the away teams? Now work out the average number of goals scored by the home teams and the average number scored by the away teams.

Cross-curricular values

Self-esteem

Scott practised his football until he was good. Take the opportunity, perhaps in a Circle Time, to ask the children to think of something they are good at. They could do this in pairs, which would give you the opportunity to move round the pairs and make suggestions. You need to ensure that every child has something they are able to claim that they are good at.

Go round the circle and each child names one thing they are good at.

Now ask the children to name something they would like to improve on. Enter an agreement that for one month they will practise this thing often, working hard. One month later, perhaps again in Circle Time, the children could report back on the progress they made.

Cooperation

The class could work together on a huge football picture for the classroom wall. Use a large poster-sized piece of paper. Mark out a football pitch, leaving room for a spectator stand at the back. Each child draws, on their own small piece of paper, a figure to go in the stands and these are pasted on. (At the back only the heads of the people will be seen.) Assign to the children the remaining elements of the picture (players, referee, football, advertising posters etc.). Give each child a piece of paper of the right size for their assigned element. They paint or draw this and then paste it onto the football pitch poster. Alternatively, if sufficient sports sections of newspapers are collected over a number of weeks, it may be possible for the children to cut out the players from their favourite team and paste them onto the pitch in the appropriate position. It may be impossible to achieve a full team of cut-outs; a panorama of dramatic moments would be equally effective.

Cooperation and bullying

Alternatively (or additionally) the children can cooperate on an anti-bullying poster. Explain that in the story Scott was called names and was attacked. (Name calling is a form of bullying.) Bullying is cowardly because the bully picks on someone who is weaker or smaller who can't fight back.

At the top of a large poster-sized sheet write, No Bullying Here.

Give each child a blank postcard.

Ask the children to remember the story about Alpha the water-zeddar and all the beautiful natural creatures and objects which they thought about (e.g. otters, tigers, flowers, rainbows etc.). Each child chooses and paints one of these beautiful things on their card.

The cards are pasted on the poster sheet to form a frame.

With the children, brainstorm suggestions about how to stop bullying in their classroom, playground or school. With younger children the teacher will write the suggestions onto the poster. Older children could write their own suggestion for themselves.

Interdisciplinary activities

An anti-bullying assembly

An anti-bullying theme would be a good choice for a school assembly and would bring in creative writing, music and song, moral and spiritual values.

Photocopiable page 47 provides a fully planned assembly on this theme.

The children can practise and use this assembly and/or use this as a model to construct an assembly using stories, poems and prayers written by the children and incorporating their own choice of an appropriate hymn or song.

Games

Children learn and practise a range of interdisciplinary skills through play. The football topic provides an ideal opportunity to allow the children some game sessions which they will see as great fun.

The interdisciplinary areas drawn into the game playing and game construction include literacy (telling/writing and following instructions), numeracy (implicit in many dice and card games), memory (a cross-curricular ability), art and design, and technology.

KS1

Teach the children to play the memory card game of *fish*. The cards are spread out face downwards. The player turns over any two. If they match in number, the player wins the pair and turns over two more and so on until he or she mismatches and replaces the mismatched pair face downwards exactly where they were picked up from. The winner is the player who wins the largest number of matched pairs. Obviously remembering where the different numbered cards are is a winning strategy. Using several packs of cards will enable the children to play in small groups.

Allow older children to bring in some favourite board games. You could organise a game champion competition.

KS2

Designing your own game of snakes and ladders.

Give each child a photocopy of resource page 48. (These could be copied onto thin card.) The children draw their own picture, perhaps of a football scene, though they could choose to do an abstract pattern. They should use soft crayons or coloured pencils so as not to obscure the numbered squares. The children weave into their picture about three ladders of different length and about three snakes, also of different lengths. They then write instructions for playing snakes and ladders and paste these on the back of their game.

Gifted children could try to invent their own new game using the same number grid provided.

FIGURE 3.2

FOOTBALL SCORES

Home team	Score	Away team	Score
Birmingham	1	Fulham	0
Burnley	1	Aston Villa	1
Chelsea	4	Wolves	0
Hull	3	West Ham	3
Liverpool	0	Man City	0
Man Utd	5	Everton	2
Sunderland	5	Arsenal	4

Anti-bullying assembly

(A planned assembly to follow or adapt)

Introduce the theme

Today we are thinking about bullying, which includes hitting, pinching, pushing, name calling and ignoring. Bullying is wrong because it is unkind and cowardly.
(Who will introduce the assembly? What else could they say about bullying?)

The story

Read 'The Beautiful Game'
or
The children write a story about bullying. The best is chosen and used in the assembly.

The poem

The teacher and children choose a poem about bullying. For example, 'Who's a Bully?' in *Poems for Circle Time and Literacy Hour* (M. Goldthorpe, LDA).
There are also several suitable poems in *Poems about You and Me: A Collection of Poems about Values* (B. Moses, Wayland Publishing).
or
The children write a poem about bullying. More than one could be read in the assembly.

Song

'Seeds of Kindness', no. 42 in *Every Colour under the Sun* (Ward Lock Educational).
or
The children work in groups of four to six to select an appropriate song from the school song books and then vote on which one to use.

Quiet reflection (or prayer)

Close your eyes and remember when someone was kind to you. (Pause.) Resolve to be kind to someone today. Now think about this assembly – the story and poems and song. (Pause.) Decide never to bully and if possible to help those who are bullied. Finally let us think about and be thankful for all the caring, kind people in the world.
or
The children write a quiet reflection (or prayer). The teacher selects one of these for the assembly.

70	51	50	31	30	11	10
69	52	49	32	29	12	9
68	53	48	33	28	13	8
67	54	47	34	27	14	7
66	55	46	35	26	15	6
65	56	45	36	25	16	5
64	57	44	37	24	17	4
63	58	43	38	23	18	3
62	59	42	39	22	19	2
61	60	41	40	21	20	1

4

Terror in the tunnel

Topics and themes

The boy-friendly topic for this chapter is terrorism and the universal theme is running from danger. The story is about a deaf girl and her brother who must escape from school bombers. The resources provide disability-aware and encryption/decoding activities.

Literacy development

Introduce the story vocabulary in your usual way.

Read the story yourself but vary subsequent readings – the children reading aloud in turn or reading to themselves.

Talking about the story and the literacy activities provided aim to develop oracy, reading skills and practice in a variety of writing forms.

Subject areas

Maths, Literacy, Art

Cross-curricular values

Inclusive education (i.e. disability awareness)

Interdisciplinary projects

Link project

Suggested resources

One photocopiable page is provided

Books

Fiction

The Boy's Book of Spycraft: How to Be the Best Secret Agent Ever, M. Oliver (Buster Books)
The Owl Who Was Afraid of the Dark: Sing a Story, J. Tomlinson and P. Howard (Egmont Books)
Special Stories for Disability Awareness, M. Leicester (Jessica Kingsley)

Non-fiction

Codes: How to Make 'Em and Break 'Em, K. Poskett (Scholastic)
British Sign Language: A Beginner's Guide, D. Miles (BBC Books)
Creating an Inclusive School, M. Leicester (Continuum)

Web Sites

www.encyclopedia.kids.net.au/page/en/Enigma
www.britishsignlanguage.com/

Other

Obtain a school or local library bulk library loan of children's adventure novels

Vocabulary

Lip-read	Know what someone is saying by how their mouth moves making words
Row	Noise
Deserted	Empty
Loitering	Hanging about
Hearing people	People who can hear, are not deaf
Disappointed	Feeling let down
Menacingly	Threateningly
Fled	Ran away quickly
Drawbridge	Bridge that swings up

Towpath	Path by canal originally used by a horse pulling (towing) a barge
Stranded	Left behind
Furious	Very angry
Alleged	Claimed but unproved
Evidence	Items found by police to prove something
Confident	Sure
Conviction	Finding someone guilty
A piece of cake	Easy

The story

Terror in the tunnel

I lip-read Dad's words. I could tell he was angry.

'I can't work with all this row. Go and play outside. Now!'

It was a cold, grey day. Ryan and I put on our coats and walked to the local playground, which was deserted except for two big boys loitering by the gate. They stopped talking as we went in and one, who was wearing a black hoodie, turned his face away.

Ryan and I walked to the bench at the far side.

'You know what, Lucy, Dad's always shouting these days, about how much noise we make,' Ryan said.

I grinned. 'I've noticed that you hearing people often find the world too noisy! Actually, Mum says he's worried about money. He has to finish this job quickly. We're broke. That's why we can't hire a canal boat this year.'

'That's not fair!' said Ryan. 'He knows how much you love your silent boat rides.'

My brother thought, wrongly, that I minded about being deaf but he was right about the boat. I loved gliding on the water and watching the fields and the trees slide by. I was disappointed about it.

I found myself blinking back tears and turned my face away from Ryan, looking over to the big kids by the gate and, without really meaning to, I lip-read what one of them was saying.

'We got away with it and we've got enough stuff to make another. We'll leave it in the swimming bath lockers next time.'

I froze. Five days ago someone had planted a bomb in the bike shed at the secondary school. It had killed two kids and injured five others. On the news it had said that the police thought the bomber was known to the school. I touched Ryan's arm.

'They're the school bombers,' I signed.

'What! Those two!' he blurted, startled.

The two boys had heard him. I saw them look over. They began to move towards us menacingly, and I could see the glint of a knife in the hooded boy's left hand.

FIGURE 4.1 Terror in the tunnel 1.

Ryan and I fled. We climbed over the fence and ran into the trees behind it. We slipped and slithered down towards the canal and squeezed through a gap in the fence along the towpath. *Good*, I thought. *It's too narrow for the bombers.*

We ran towards the tunnel. It's for the boats, but this one had a narrow wooden footpath on one side. I'm scared of tunnels and Dad always plans our route to avoid them. Frightened, I followed Ryan into the pitch dark. With one hand on the rough slimy wall I shuffled my way along, scared of rats or snakes or gaps in the rickety wood.

We inched forward and I jumped when I felt heavy drops of cold water hit my head and soak into my coat. The walkway became wet and slippery and I was scared we might fall into the cold, black water.

For a long time we moved slowly through the darkness. I was shivering through fear and from the icy cold and from knowing that I wouldn't hear the killers coming up behind me. Every moment I expected to feel a knife in my back and to drop into the canal and drown.

At last we saw a glimmer of light at the far end and slowly, very gradually, this grew bigger until we were outside, blinking in the bright air.

We ran on along the towpath. Glancing over my shoulder I saw the bombers behind us. Side by side, my brother and I ran as fast as we could. The killers were gaining on us. I saw a man ahead, on the other side of the canal. He was opening the drawbridge so that his boat could pass through. The gap between the drawbridge and the towpath was widening.

Desperately I jumped the gap, with Ryan just a split second behind me. We rolled down the slope of the bridge, landing at the other side of the water. I saw that the man was yelling at us. We scrambled to our feet. The bombers, stranded on the other side, were looking furious.

Ryan and I ran away from the canal and through the car park of a canalside pub. We found ourselves in Wharf Road, a busy street of fast traffic. As we pounded along the pavement I saw Ryan speaking into his mobile phone.

We turned left into a street lined with houses. Ryan pulled me after him down someone's path. We crossed two gardens and in the next street doubled back to the road with the pub.

'Ryan, they might see us,' I said. 'We should hide.' Ryan stopped and looked into my face.

'Keep on the lookout for them, Lucy,' he told me. 'The thing is I phoned home and Mum is sending Dad and the police to find us in Wharf Road.'

Fortunately, in Wharf Road, a police car quickly pulled up beside us. A window was lowered.

'You the Williamson twins?' the policeman asked.

'Yes,' Ryan answered.

'Well, where are these alleged bombers?' he said to us, and then, shouting over our shoulders, 'Hey you two lads, come here!'

I looked round and saw the two bombers turning to run away. Two policemen jumped out of the car and gave chase. It was exciting to watch. They caught the bombers and marched them back.

Suddenly Dad's car arrived and screeched to a stop. Dad jumped out and pulled Ryan and me into a crushing hug, one in each arm.

We all had to go to the police station. Ryan and I made statements. It took ages. It was well after lunch when we got home and we were starving. Mum hugged us with tears streaming down her face. Instead of our usual healthy sandwich, she made us bacon, egg, beans and masses of chips.

A week later a policeman and woman came round. They told us that they had found all the evidence they needed at each of the houses of the two bombers. They were confident of a conviction and to our delight Ryan and I were entitled to a reward. I couldn't believe how much it was.

'That's twenty times the cost of hiring a canal boat,' Dad said. 'Well done you two. We can hire a boat after all!'

'Yes,' said Mum. 'And this year we'll have two weeks instead of one.'

'And this year let's try the tunnel route.' I reached for a piece of Mum's chocolate gâteau. 'After walking through a tunnel in the dark, sailing through with lights on will be a piece of cake.'

© Mal Leicester

Literacy development

Talking about the story

- Why did Lucy need to lip-read Dad's words?

- Why couldn't the family have their canal boat holiday that year?

- In what way was going through the tunnel scary?

- How did Lucy and Ryan get across the canal away from the bombers?

- Why did Lucy and Ryan get a reward?

Points for discussion

- What did Lucy like about canal boat trips? What do you enjoy about your holidays?

- What do the children know about sign language?

- Have any of the children been on a canal boat? What creatures did they see?

Literacy activities

Reading and review project

Visit the school or local library or make use of the bulk library loan. Let the children choose an exciting adventure book. After reading the book they must do a review. First explain the difference between *plot* (what happens) and *theme* (what the story is about, e.g. courage).

The review must include:

- The plot. Do not give the ending away!

- Discussion of the theme

- About the main character(s)

- If possible, comparison of this book with other books you have read

- Why did you like it (or not)?

Good reviews can be read aloud to the class so that the children will be encouraged to try other adventure books which other children have enjoyed.

An escape story

Let the children draw or write a story entitled 'The Escape'. Many adventure stories involve the quest to escape in the midst of danger and excitement. The children should make their story as exciting as possible.

Subject-centred activities

Art

Canal art

Show the children pictures of canal art. Let the children draw the outline of a canal boat or a big jug and, using thick bright paint, have them decorate it with a flower design.

Movement

Give the children a copy of photocopiable page 59. Discuss how the illustrator has drawn the two figures in movement, jumping across the gap as the drawbridge begins to rise. They should illustrate their own story ('The Escape'), showing their hero in action. The children should try to depict movement.

Maths: codes

A simple code

Explain the simple code in which A = 1, B = 2, C = 3 etc. Give the children the photocopiable page. Can they work out the first message?

Let the children go on to create a slightly more complicated code and write a message of their own. For example, Z = 1, Y = 2, X = 3 etc. or A = 11, B = 12, C = 13 etc.

Can the children work out each other's codes and read some messages?

Difficult codes

If you devise your code from a secret sentence it becomes very difficult to break it. For example, for message (2) on the photocopiable page we have devised a code based on the last sentence of the chapter story.

A	f	t	e	r	w	a	l	k	i	n	g	t	h	r	o	u	g	h	a	t	u	n	n	e	l	i	n	t	h	e
1	2	3	4	5	6		7	8	9	10	11		12		13	14		15												

d	a	r	k	s	a	i	l	l	i	n	g	t	h	r	o	u	g	h	w	i	t	h	l	i	g	h	t	s	o	n
16			17																											

FIGURE 4.2 Difficult codes.

Cross-curricular values

Inclusive education (i.e. disability awareness, empathy, kindness)

Prejudice and discrimination against disabled people is widespread and it is part of multicultural/diversity/equality in education to encourage more positive attitudes and greater understanding in your pupils. Seek out people, resources, literature, activities etc. to promote an inclusive education. Here are two suggestions to help and which will link into the story.

1   Deaf people often get left out of conversations by hearing people because we don't take the trouble to face them (for lip-reading) or to learn Sign Language. The children will find it fun to learn some sign language and to practise some simple conversations.

2   Lucy was deaf. What would that be like? What are the good things about being deaf (for example, enjoying beautiful sights without noisy distractions, learning how to lip-read and see secret conversations, having two languages – English and Sign Language – not being distracted by unpleasant or loud noise especially when trying to sleep or work)? What are the bad things (for example, not hearing music, missing out on conversations in hearing groups)?

The children could write a story with a deaf hero or heroine, reflecting some of these experiences. Perhaps their hero or heroine could foil a criminal plot by lip-reading what the criminals are saying.

You could repeat this exercise with a hero who has some other impairment (for example, blindness, mobility problems etc.).

Interdisciplinary activities

Link project

Linking a special school with a mainstream school for a common project can be a good learning experience for the children of both schools. Such link projects need to be properly prepared for but can work well.

See A. Lewis (1985) *Children's Understanding of Disability* (London: Routledge).

FIGURE 4.3 Terror in the tunnel 2.

Codes

Message One

14	15	23		13	1	11	5		15	23	14		3	15	4	5

Message Two

6	4	7	7		16	13	10	4		3	12	9	17		6	1	17		15	1	5	16

5

The evil ghost of Castle Chameleon

Topics and themes

The boy-friendly topic for this chapter is ghosts and the universal theme is the supernatural with, therefore, a focus on critical thinking. The story is about a boy who must recapture an evil apparition. The resources provide ghostly activities and learning exercises to develop the skills of critical thinking.

Literacy development

Introduce the story vocabulary in your usual way.

Read the story yourself but vary subsequent readings – the children reading aloud in turn or reading to themselves.

Talking about the story and the literacy activities provided aim to develop oracy, reading skills and practice in a variety of writing forms.

Subject areas

History – castles: see web sites on resource page and books listed for a wealth of material with activities

Introduction to philosophy

Cross-curricular thinking skills

Critical thinking

Interdisciplinary projects

Media studies
Moral reflection

Suggested resources

One photocopiable page is provided

Books

Fiction

Roald Dahl's Book of Ghosts, R. Dahl (Perfect)
The Harry Potter books, J. K. Rowling (Scholastic)
Castle Diary: The Diary of Tobias Burgess, R. Platt (Candlewick)

Non-fiction

Knights and Castle: 50 Hands-On Activities to Experience the Middle Ages, H. Avery and P. Mantell (Kaleidoscope Kids)
Developing Critical Thinking Skills, M. Leicester (Continuum)
The Philosophy Gym, S. Law (Orion)
101+ Ideas for Teaching Thinking Skills, S. Bowkett (Continuum)

Web sites

www.ks1resources.co.uk/page149.html
www.royalcollection.org.uk/default.asp?action=article&ID=231

Vocabulary

Naughty	Doing mischievous things
Constant	All the time
Grumpy	Bad tempered
Old-fashioned	From the past, not modern
Bored	Fed up
On impulse	Without thinking, on the spur of the moment
Forbidden	Not allowed
Approaching	Coming nearer
Evil	Bad, wicked
Malevolent	Evil
Exasperation	Feeling vexed

Amazement	Surprise
Floating	Moving slowly in air or water
Sympathetic	Feel sorry for, understand
Swiftly	Quickly
Benevolent	Kind, good
Ajar	Open
Procession	One after the other
Apparition	Ghostly being
Terror	Fear
Shimmering	Glowing

The story

The evil ghost of Castle Chameleon

'Gran's not feeling well today, Will,' Mum said.

'Oh no!' said Will. 'I suppose Ali will have to come with us.'

Mum nodded. 'She won't be any trouble. You'll see.'

'Yeah, yeah, yeah,' said Will. He knew his naughty little sister would spoil everything.

On the way to Castle Chameleon Ali never stopped talking. Not once. Not for a second. Yak, yak, yak. A constant stream of talk. Will didn't listen. He stared out of the car window feeling grumpy. The castle was made of grey stone and had turrets at each corner. The decorated edges at the top of the castle made it look like a huge wedding cake.

'That square shape is called castellated,' said Mum. 'And the castle is called Castle Chameleon because, in the rain, its grey stone turns blue.'

'Will it change now?' asked Ali.

'It's not raining now, silly,' said Will.

'Why is it not raining?' asked Ali.

'Oh put a sock in it,' said Will.

Once inside Castle Chameleon, Will enjoyed trying out the old-fashioned toys in the play-room. Mum let him stay there on his own, taking Ali with her into the room next door. After a while, however, Will began to get bored. He decided to find Mum. He went out of the play-room and noticed that a yellow rope was stretched across the opposite corridor. A Keep Out sign was attached to the rope. *I wonder why*, he thought.

On impulse Will ducked under the rope and walked down the forbidden way. He heard the sharp tap of high-heeled shoes approaching towards the yellow rope. Not wanting to be seen behind the Keep Out sign he stepped into a small alcove to hide.

As the footsteps drew nearer Will tensed and held his breath, hoping that whoever it was would not turn into the roped off corridor. He leaned back in relief when he heard the steps go by.

Now Will's head pressed against the carved wall behind him and he heard a click. He found himself falling backwards. A door, cleverly disguised in the

FIGURE 5.1 The evil ghost.

carving, had swung inward and he stumbled in with it. He steadied himself. He was inside a dark, windowless room. The light spilling in from the corridor revealed it to be shaped like a coffin – a large empty coffin. However, as Will's eyes grew used to the darkness he discovered that in fact the room was not empty at all. He stood rigid with fear. He could just make out a faint shape in the corner: a tall figure in the robes of a monk with round holes for his eyes and a screaming mouth like a Halloween mask.

The figure glided towards Will. He stepped back into the lighted corridor and felt the thing brush past, as soft and cold as a breeze. He shivered. The thing itself seemed to become invisible in the bright light outside. Had he really seen it? An evil ghost? A malevolent monk?

Will fled, back to the yellow rope. Ducking under, he passed the play-room and found Mum still in the next one along. She was listening to a boring man talking about the dark oil paintings on the walls. Ali was asleep in her pushchair, which had been parked in a corner of the room.

Will whispered to his Mum about the escaped ghost but she only laughed.

'What a vivid imagination you have,' she said.

Will rolled his eyes up in exasperation and, to his alarm and amazement, he saw the ghost above him, floating in a corner near the ceiling. The ghost gave an evil smile and began to swing a heavy light shade, the end one in a diagonal row – an end one directly above his sleeping sister.

Will sprang across the room and grabbed the handle of the pushchair, pulling it towards him. The heavy glass shade crashed to the ground, smashing just on the spot where Ali had been.

The noise of the crash woke her and she started to howl. Usually Will hated the sound of his sister's crying but this time he felt sympathetic. He almost felt like crying himself.

Mum was staring in astonishment, taking in what had happened.

'Oh Will, you saved her from that heavy light. You acted so swiftly. You were brilliant. A hero.'

Mum began to comfort Ali, who continued to sob.

'Mum, let's go out to the maze,' Will said. He wanted to get them all away from the ghost.

At the maze Mum and Ali followed Will as he managed to find his way to the centre. There they found a large, flat stone with a poem carved into the top.

Lay aside your trembling fear
Wipe away your trembling tear
Stand in that room not far from here
The coffin room so near and drear
Summon the monk with this song
Benevolence, benevolence
Summon the monk to save the young
Benevolence, benevolence
Stand your ground until he's found
Slam the door for evermore
Your good and brave benevolence
Defeats the monk's malevolence

'What a strange verse. Whatever can it mean?' said Mum.

Will knew. With a sinking feeling in his stomach he realised what he must do. He must return to the coffin room. He must chant the word 'benevolence' until the evil ghost returned. He must not run away until the monk was inside. Will shuddered. The two of them must be in the coffin room together.

'Wait here, Mum', he said, 'And keep Ali safe with you.'

Before Mum could stop him Will raced back to the castle, ran up the grand stairway and back to the yellow rope. He ducked under and ran to the coffin-shaped room. The door gaped ajar. Trembling, Will stepped inside. A cold wind seemed to blow about him, a howling filled his ears, a pungent smell attacked his nose. Will licked his lips, which were dry with fear. He wanted to run but forced himself to remain.

A procession of ghostly images appeared and swirled about him before disappearing into the darkness – a spider monster with the head of a dead man, a woman with the staring yellow eyes of a tiger, a baby doll which opened its mouth to show pointed teeth dripping with blood. With each apparition Will wanted to flee, but he stood his ground and chanted, 'benevolence, benevolence'. Eventually the malevolent monk swirled into the room. He cast a look of fury at Will.

'Benevolence, benevolence,' chanted Will.

The ghost moved towards him. Will stood his ground.

'Benevolence, benevolence,' chanted Will.

With a look of terror the malevolent monk began to dwindle and shrink.

'Benevolence, benevolence,' chanted Will.

The malevolent monk shrank down until he was completely gone. Will stepped out of the coffin room and slammed the door.

Will raced back outside to his Mum and Ali.

'My dear you look so pale. Wherever have you been?' Mum hugged Will. 'My Castle Chameleon hero. You saved your sister's life. Wait till we tell Dad.'

'Is he a superhero?' said Ali and Will grinned. Sometimes Ali wasn't so bad after all.

Just then it began to rain. Mum put up her umbrella and the three of them stood together under it. Through the pouring rain, they gazed at Castle Chameleon, which slowly changed from a dull grey to a shimmering, beautiful blue.

© Mal Leicester

Literacy development

Talking about the story

- Why was Will grumpy at the beginning?

- Why was the castle called Castle Chameleon?

- Why did Will go under the Keep Out rope?

- Did Mum believe in the ghost?

- How did the evil ghost try to hurt Ali?

- What scary things did Will see in the coffin-shaped room?

Points for discussion

- Do you think Will loved his little sister? Is there a difference between love and like?

- Does the ghost exist for real in the story?

- Do you believe in ghosts in real life? What reasons do you have?

- Mum described Will as her Castle Chameleon hero? Do you think Will was a hero? (Why?)

Literacy activities

Give the children a photocopy of page 73. Ask them to colour in the ghost's white eyes and mouth and the white edging of his robes, choosing a colour they think most scary, and colour Will's clothing using their favourite colours.

KS1

Draw a scary ghost of your own. Draw or write a story about him.

KS2

The children write their own ghost story trying to make it scary.

Subject-centred activities

Introduction to philosophy

Some schools introduce children to philosophy because it is an area which children find interesting. They often ask big questions about why things are as they are. Philosophical questions cannot be answered by facts. They are questions which call for reflection. They are thus good questions for encouraging criticality or critical reflection. Here are some questions to set the children thinking. Introduce some of them, and discuss them with the class.

1   How do I know that I am not dreaming this classroom?

2   Did God create the universe?

3   Could a God who is good have created this world which has evil in it?

4   Why do we exist? What is the meaning of life?

5   What is the difference between education and indoctrination?

6   Do we each have a mind, a body and a soul?

7   How can I know that you feel pain like I feel pain?

8   Do you see colours like I see colours?

9   What is happiness?

10   How do I know what is the right thing to do?

Cross-curricular thinking skills

Critical thinking skills

Critical thinking skills cross the curriculum. Critical thinking involves *critical reflection*, including the ability to question assumptions, notice context and see alternatives. All this helps you to form your own point of view, an informed viewpoint. The kind of questions will be different in the different areas of knowledge but the reflective stance is common to all subject areas. Similarly, *being rational* is about having sound reasons and evidence for your beliefs, together with being able to see that an argument is sound/logical but what counts as evidence varies. (For example, in science as distinct from in literature.) The habits of seeking and noticing justifications, and giving reasons, are habits of thinking to be cultivated across the curriculum. Tools of reflection such as *meta-analysis* also bring thinking to a higher level in all areas of the curriculum. The activities suggested practise these cognitive skills.

- Memory and imagination: ask the children to write a brief account of some event that they remember. Now ask them to write an imaginary event which happens in the same place. Ask them to compare the way they went about preparing these tasks. When the children read out their accounts, can the group tell which is which? They must give reasons for what they say.

- Point of view: the children write a dialogue of a quarrel between two different characters. One character is a boy and one character is a girl. First they write the quarrel from the boy's point of view. Second they write the same quarrel but from the girl's point of view.

- Thinking of alternatives: the children could be inventors. Ask them to invent and design a new toy or game.

- Detective story: the children could write a detective story so that they have to think about what would count as evidence, what kind of thing the detective looks for. (You could precede this by reading some detective stories with the children.)

- Arrange a debate: choose a topic that the children will find of interest or allow the children to choose a topic. Arrange a formal debate with a proposer and an opposer and a seconder for each. Chair questions/discussions that follow the short presentations. A debate is a good way of making the children arrange their thoughts and back them up with reasons and consider different points of view.

Questioning: encourage the children to be questioning and reflective, to ask questions such as: Do I agree/disagree with what is being argued? Why? Is it plausible? Is it backed by good evidence? How much evidence is there for the opposite point of view? What assumptions are being made?

- A controversial topic: older children could research a controversial topic. They then write a piece giving an introduction (what is the topic and why is it important and controversial), presenting one point of view with reasons and evidence, presenting the opposite point of view with reasons and evidence, and as a conclusion presenting their own point of view with their reasons and evidence.

- Category making: start with a specific object and see if the children can categorise it into increasingly general groups. For example:

  - pan handle → pan → kitchen utensil → handmade artefact

  or

  - cat → pet → mammal → animal → living creature

  Or go from the general to the more specific. For example:

  - vehicle → car → racing car → Formula 1 car

- Find and name groups: provide a jumble of names of objects which they must sort into categories. Any that do not fit can be labelled miscellaneous or oddments. You could arrive at the initial list of objects by writing suggestions from each member of your class.

- Make comparisons: take two separate objects and see how many similarities and differences the children can find, for example sea and sand, school and restaurant.

Interdisciplinary activities

Media studies

Studying the media with children is a good way to encourage their critical thinking skills.

Ask the children to select and bring in a selection of advertisements cut from newspapers and magazines. If it is possible, you should also record some TV ads and show these in class. The children can analyse the magazine and TV ads using their critical thinking skills. This can be done as whole class or in smaller groups. Remind them to look for hidden assumptions, dubious claims without any evidence, sweeping statements that may not be true and so on.

You could follow this critical work by allowing the children to design an advert of their own. They should aim to create a visual design with a catch phrase to create a positive, persuasive image of something they are trying to sell!

Moral reflection

We often have to apply critical thinking to moral dilemmas, trying to answer the question, 'What ought I to do?'

Moral problems are those concerned with good and evil, with how we can do the right thing.

Ask the children what moral problems they have faced. You will have to explain what you mean and give some examples. When you have got three or four moral dilemmas, write these on the board and use each one as a basis for a class discussion. Some additional discussion possibilities might be:

- Does David Beckham deserve to be paid so much money?

- What you cannot afford you should steal from others

- Never start a fight but defend yourself if you are attacked

- Help other people when you can

- Keep your promises

- Take as much of everything as you can get

(Remind the children that we need to behave as we would want others to behave. They can ask themselves, what if everyone did this?)

Belief in ghosts

In the story we accepted that there was an evil ghost in Castle Chameleon. Discuss the existence of ghosts with the children. Encourage the children to see that there is no sound evidence for the existence of ghosts. Discuss when someone sees a ghost how many other explanations there could be for what they saw. Do you believe in ghosts? Why/why not? The children could have a debate about the existence of ghosts. Then the children write a piece explaining what they believe about ghosts and why.

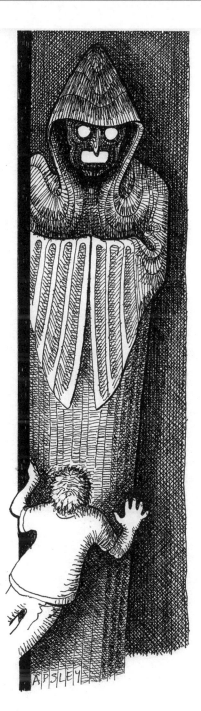

FIGURE 5.2 In the coffin-shaped room.

6

Percy's big adventure

Topics and themes

The boy-friendly topic for this chapter is cars in all their variety, including classic, vintage and veteran cars, and the universal themes are the desire for adventure and empathetic kindness. The story is about Percy Riley, a 1934 Riley Kestrel who travels to Le Mans in France and helps Bébé, a 1912 Peugeot. The resources provide car-related activities that are both educative and fun.

Literacy development/English

Introduce the story vocabulary in your usual way.

Read the story yourself but vary subsequent readings – the children reading aloud in turn or reading to themselves.

Talking about the story and the literacy activities provided aim to develop oracy, reading skills and practice in a variety of writing forms.

Other subject areas

History, Art

Cross-curricular values

Empathy
Kindness
Courage

Interdisciplinary projects

Designing a car/understanding the features of a car

Suggested resources

Four photocopiable pages are provided

Books

Fiction

The Thomas the Tank Engine series, Rev. W. Awdry (Egmont)
The Cosy Park Garage Series, M. Leicester and R. Twelvetrees (Inky Fingers)
The Gumdrop series, Val Biro (Hodder)
The Mister Men series, R. Hargreaves (Egmont)

Non-fiction

Cars, D. Glover and P. Glover (Wayland)
Sports Cars, P. Worms (Motormania)
My Best Book about Cars, anon. (Ladybird)

Web sites

Vintage Sports Car Club: www.vscc.co.uk/vsccweb/
Veteran Car Club of GB: www.vccofgb.co.uk/
Thousands of online images of early motor racing: www.brooklands.org.uk/
Online magazine: www.prewarcar.com/

Other

Local car/transport museums

Vocabulary

Adventure	Exciting and possibly dangerous journey
Anniversary	A time when an event that happened a number of years ago is remembered
Channel Tunnel	A tunnel under the English Channel that trains go through carrying cars, lorries and people
Parade	Everyone marching or driving along a road together
Sinking	Going down
Bitterly	Very sadly

Stranded	On your own in a place that you cannot get away from
Examined	Looked very carefully at
Plastered	Thickly covered
Au revoir	Goodbye in French
Spellbound	Listening with very great interest

Car-related vocabulary

Rileys	Cars made by the Riley car company in Coventry
Racing track	A road made specially for cars to race
Mulsanne Straight	A famous section of the Le Mans twenty-four-hour race track where the highest speeds are reached
Toot	A sound from a car horn
Balilla	A two-seater sports car
Fiat	Italian car maker based in Turin (Fabbrica Italiana Automobili Torino)
Full throttle	Accelerator pedal right down to the floor
Exhaust	Pipe from the engine to the back of the car where sound and gases come out
70 mph	Seventy miles per hour. Normal motorway speed limit (very fast for a 1934 car)
Oil	Substance in engine to make the moving parts slip and slide easily
Sign posts	Notices placed at road junctions to show drivers where the roads go
Beaulieu Autojumble	A very large open market where vintage cars and parts for vintage cars are sold

The story

Percy's big adventure
Book Four of the Cosy Park Garage Series

Mr Fettler smiled at Percy. 'Today's your big adventure, Percy.'

All his life Percy Riley had longed for an adventure. He'd never had one before, but, now that it was here, he was scared. He smiled back at Mr Fettler so that no one would guess how frightened he was.

Ruby looked puzzled. 'Tell me again, Percy,' she said.

'It's the anniversary of Riley's racing success at Le Mans in France, and we Riley cars will take part in the victory parade.'

All his friends crowded into the doorway to watch Percy drive off. None of the cars had been out of England before. Percy could see them flashing farewell with their lights.

Percy gave a cheerful toot on his horn but deep in his engine he was worried. Le Mans was a very long way. *I might get lost. I might break down. I might never get home again.*

First Percy had to drive round London. It began to pour with rain, and he could hardly see. Huge lorries thundered by, covering him with spray. It was scary. Percy continued onward to the Channel Tunnel, where he drove onto the train which was to carry him under the sea to France. He stood in a line of other cars, secretly scared of the tunnel. *Do sea monsters live there?* he wondered. When the train started up he saw only the strong tunnel walls speeding by. He began to feel better.

At the other end of the tunnel, Percy drove into France. He followed signs for Le Mans. Anxious not to miss the parade Percy drove on and on and on without ever stopping for a rest.

At last he arrived and enjoyed himself with the other Rileys. He drove proudly round the racing track, speeding up along the Mulsanne Straight. *What a great adventure,* he thought.

That night Percy slept well and the next morning he set off for England feeling pleased with himself. He pictured telling his friends about the parade. A toot from behind brought him out of his daydream. It was Balilla, the cheeky little Fiat.

'How about a race, Percy?'

FIGURE 6.1 Bébé.

'Right,' shouted Percy, going full throttle. His exhaust boomed and his whole body shivered with excitement. Ahead was a long, straight, tree-lined road. He speeded up, and by 70 mph Percy's six-cylinder engine was singing with delight. Percy and the Fiat were still wheel to wheel. Then, with a broad grin, Percy raced ahead, leaving the Fiat behind in a cloud of dust.

He drove on, even more pleased with himself until, with a sinking feeling in the pit of his engine, he realised his oil was leaking. *A pipe has come loose in that race. Will the oil run out before I get home,* he worried?

A few miles down the road Percy saw a traffic light on red. He slowed and stopped. He noticed the pretty French car in front. She was weeping bitterly.

'Whatever is the matter?' he asked.

'I'm lost,' she wailed, 'and I can't read these sign posts. I don't know how I will ever find my way home.'

Percy forgot his own worries.

'I can read the signs. I'll show you the way.'

'Oh thank you, Monsieur. I'm Bébé Peugeot from Percy, by the way.'

FIGURE 6.2 Percy.

'From Percy! I'm Percy too! Percy Riley from England.'

Percy followed the signs for *Percy,* his fear rising as his oil level dropped. He imagined himself stranded in France. He should make for home before his oil ran out. *But I must help Bébé,* he thought.

Percy's oil ran out just as he reached Bébé's garage.

'No oil! Oh Bébé! I'll never get home now. Whatever shall I do?'

'Don't worry, Percy, I'm sure Madame Fettleur will help you.'

Percy blinked in surprise and sudden hope.

'You have Madame Fettleur to look after you, Bébé?'

Madame Fettleur examined Percy's engine, which was plastered in oil. Percy waited anxiously.

'I'll soon stop that leak and replace your oil,' she said. She worked hard.

'That's it. You're ready to go home now, Percy.'

Percy gave a huge sigh of relief. 'Thank you, Madame Fettleur.'

FIGURE 6.3 Percy at Le Mans.

'Goodbye, Percy,' said Bébé. 'Thank you so much.' She smiled into his headlights and gave his wheels a soft nudge with her own.

'Au revoir, Bébé,' said Percy.

After that Percy journeyed back home. It was a happy journey. His oil no longer leaked and his worries had leaked away instead.

Back at Cosy Park Mr Fettler and the cars gathered round him.

'Tell us all about it,' they said.

First he told them about the journey to Le Mans and about driving down the Mulsanne Straight.

'Splendid,' said Mr Fettler.

Second he told them about winning the race with the Fiat and about leaking his oil.

The cars listened spellbound.

Third he told them about helping Bébé to find her way home.

'Oh how romantic,' breathed Ruby. 'I never thought you would have such a big adventure.'

'I was scared at times,' Percy admitted, 'but it was worth it.'

His friends nodded. 'Yes, it was worth it Percy,' they all said.

'Madame Fettleur and Bébé will be at the Beaulieu Autojumble next month Mr Fettler. I'd like to go and see them.'

'Certainly, Percy,' said Mr Fettler. 'You've done well.'

Percy didn't know where Beaulieu was, but he knew he would find it. He wasn't a bit worried. He smiled. He was happier than he had ever been in his life.

© Mal Leicester & Roger Twelvetrees

Literacy development

Talking about the story

- Where is Percy going to in France?
- What does he drive through to get to France?
- Who did Percy race with?
- How did he help Bébé?
- What went wrong for Percy?
- Who helped Percy to get home?

Points for discussion

- Why do you think people want adventures?
- Have any of the children been to a foreign country? Let them tell about this.
- Percy showed Bébé the way though his oil was leaking. Why was this especially kind?
- Why do you think Percy was really happy at the end?

Literacy activities

KS1

Talk with the children about the variety of cars today. Can they suggest different kinds of car and different kinds of features?

- Smart car

- Jaguar

- Range Rover

- Ford Mondeo

- Ferrari

   They all have different features:

- Comfortable

- Economical

- Fast

- Strong

- Small or large

- Different colours

   What kind of car will they choose when they are old enough to drive? Show the children some Mr Men books or ask them for some of the Mr Men titles. Each of the children choose one of these Mr Men (or Little Miss) and draw a car that will match their chosen character.

KS2

Give each child a photocopy of 'Prince Henry and the Wedding' (photocopiable pages 87–89). They should compare 'Percy's Big Adventure' with 'Prince Henry and the Wedding', first in discussion and then in writing, including which story they prefer and why.

   Additionally or alternatively give the children the photocopiable page of the Cosy Park characters. Some of the children will be interested to read the technical details given. The children should create their own character idea for each of the cars, which may be similar or very different from the one given on the sheet.

   Enthusiastic children could write their own car story and gifted children could write this as a story intended for very young children.

Subject-centred activities

Art

KS1

We have provided a black and white illustration of Prince Henry as a wedding car, for the children to colour in colours of their own choice. Their aim is to make the car look as attractive as possible.

History

Ask the children who has been on a steam train. Ask the children if they have ever seen a horse-drawn carriage, ridden in a carriage, seen a horse or donkey, or ridden on a horse or donkey. Explain that cars have gradually developed from the clumsy beginnings of Nicolas Cugnot's steam carriage of 1769 through the 'horseless carriage' era of the 1880s and 1890s into the 'golden age' of the 1920s and 1930s to the present day when cars have numerous safety features and cater for all the creature comforts of the passengers. For a brief history of the motor car read photocopiable page 90 with the children. NB: You may well find that a local vintage or classic car owner would be willing to visit the school with the car and answer questions from the children.

Cross-curricular values

- Empathy/kindness
- Courage

The children have already created characters/personalities to go with each of the six Cosy Park cars. Ask the children to think of one kind and one brave action which each of these characters might do. The aim is to finish up with six different kind actions and six different brave ones. Older and more able children will have a good match between characters and their actions.

Interdisciplinary projects

Talk to the children about different car features such as:

- Air bag (a bag that comes out of the dashboard and fills with air to cushion your head in a crash)

- Tinted windows (darkened glass to keep out the glare of the sun)

- Central locking (automatic locking of all doors from one key)

- Remote locking (automatic locking of the car doors by a signal from a handheld button)

- Folding roof (converts from saloon to open car at the touch of a button)

Make sure that the children understand what these five car features are. They can then decide which they would most like to have in their own car. They must give a reason for their answer. Some of the children should begin to see the difference between a simple preference (example, chocolate or ice-cream) and a preference for a reason (example, choosing the air bag because being safe is the top priority or choosing the folding roof because they love the sunshine).

What other features do some cars have? (The children should begin to understand the difference between features that all cars must have (e.g. wheels) and optional extras.)

Some features are safety features (e.g. safety belts and airbags), some are convenience features (such as remote locking) and some are comfort features (e.g. padded leather seats). Some features are aesthetic features (such as shape and colour). Some features are the essential feature which all cars must have (engine, wheels, steering wheel, brakes etc.).

Now the children design their own car. On one big sheet they:

- Draw a car to show the shape and colour

- Draw the dashboard (how will they design/organise the speedometer, petrol gauge, radio, CD player, lights etc.)

- List what features the interior would have (seating materials and colours)

- List additional safety, convenience and comfort features which their car would have

- List any points they wish to make about the car's key features: engine, steering wheel and road wheels

COSY PARK CHARACTERS

Auntie

reg no. ROV 90
1955 Rover 90 four-door
four-seat saloon
2638 cc inlet over exhaust
six-cylinder engine
top speed 90 mph

Auntie Rover is a maternal presence in Cosy Park where she is held in affection and esteem. She keeps a loving and protective eye on Bubble, Ruby, Dog and Prince Henry. Of course she is always sure that she is right. In fact she usually is. (But not always!)

Bubble

reg no. 1959 H
1959 Isetta three-wheeler
two-seater "bubble" car with
front opening door and built
in Brighton. If reverse gear
was removed it was classed
as a motorcycle.
300 cc four stroke engine
top speed 53 mph

Bubble is the youngster in Cosy Park Garage. He has little sense of danger until he lands in trouble, big time. Excitable, energetic and enthusiastic Bubble loves Dog and Morris, is great pals with Ruby and (secretly) feels safe and secure when with Auntie Rover or Landie.

Landie

reg no. SER1
1948 Series 1 Landrover
80 inch wheel base
1595 cc inlet over exhaust
four-cylinder engine
Fairey hydraulic front winch

Landie is one of the longest residents of Cosy Park Garage. He is unpretentious and down to earth. Mr Fettler relies on him a great deal and there is considerable respect between the two. Landie is also a respectful admirer of Auntie.

Morris

reg no. MOR 8
1936 Morris
two-seat Tourer
918 cc side valve engine
top speed 58 mph

Morris is the Everyman car of Cosy Park Garage. His friends know they can rely on him and from time to time he has helped each of the other cars. He is decent and kind. Dog almost invariably chooses to ride with Morris and they have a strong bond.

Prince Henry

reg no. PH 1911
1911 Vauxhall C type
Prince Henry
three-door four-seat
tourer
3053 cc side valve four-cylinder engine
Named after the Reliability Trials organised by Prince Henry of Austria in which Vauxhalls were so successful
top speed in road going form 70 mph

Aristocratic, genial and old fashioned, Prince Henry is the much loved grandfatherly figure of Cosy Park Garage. Though Henry is rather proud, he has a heart of pure gold. He is fond of all the other cars, particularly Auntie Rover and Ruby.

Ruby

reg no. AUS 7
1935 Austin Ruby
two-door
four-seat saloon
747 cc four-cylinder engine

Ruby is one of the younger members of Cosy Park. She is pretty, flighty and scatter brained. She can't help being rather vain and she likes to flirt — but not with Bubble who is her good friend. With Bubble she enjoys having a laugh.

FIGURE 6.4 Thumbnail sketches.

Prince Henry and the wedding
Book One in the Cosy Park Garage Series

'Good morning cars,' said Mr Fettler, 'I've some jobs for you today.'

'Good morning Mr Fettler,' the cars replied.

Mr Fettler sent Morris with Dog to collect flowers for a wedding at the church. He sent Auntie Rover for the huge wedding cake.

'You'll be pleased, Bubble, you can fetch my eggs from the farm.'

'Great,' squeaked Bubble and his little engine roared with excitement.

'You go too, Landie, for the milk.' said Mr Fettler. He nodded towards Bubble and gave Landie a wink.

Ah! thought old Landie, *he wants me to keep an eye on young Bubble, out on his first job*, and he winked a headlight back.

'Percy and Ruby, you're needed at Twelvetrees Farm, off you go.'

From his comfortable place next to the stove, the best place in the garage, Prince Henry looked down his fluted bonnet and watched as, one by one, the cars drove away. *I'm too important to do these little jobs,* he thought. *As everyone knows, I've carried kings and queens in my time. I've got the best place in Cosy Park. I am the grandest car.*

It was quiet when the cars had gone and, still feeling pleased with himself, Henry settled down for his morning snooze. He was just nodding off when Mr Fettler said, 'Henry, I need to tell you something. His Lordship has moved away and he won't need you now, and I'm afraid that nobody else is rich enough to buy all the petrol you drink.'

'Don't worry though, Henry, I'll not sell you for scrap. Next week you'll go and live at the Motor Museum.'

Wide awake now, Henry trembled with fear and Mr Fettler patted his bonnet.

'You'll like it there. You'll soon make new friends.'

Henry watched Mr Fettler walk away, and blinked his headlights to hold back his tears. He didn't want to leave his friends at Cosy Park. He didn't want to be parked forever in a line of silent cars. He didn't want to be stared at all day long by strangers. He wanted to stay.

He wanted to carry fine ladies and gentlemen along country lanes, hearing the sturdy *kathonka kathonka kathonka* of his big old engine booming out across the fields.

FIGURE 6.5 Prince Henry carrying the bride.

Henry was really sad. *I thought I was the best car in the garage, but I was wrong. I may be grand but I drink far too much petrol to be sent on useful jobs. Even young Bubble is more use than me.*

'Henry, what's the matter?' said a worried voice. Morris and Dog were back. Prince Henry told them about being sent away.

'Is there really no job for you, Henry?' asked Morris.

'No,' said Henry, and he watched Morris drive sadly away.

When the other cars returned, Henry told them too. Auntie Rover nudged his front wheel.

'Oh Henry my dear, we'll miss you very much.'

The circle of sad friends fell silent. Henry tried hard not to cry.

At that moment Morris roared up the street and into the garage, stopping with a screech in a cloud of smoke.

'Good news!' he shouted. 'The bride at the wedding needs a grand car to take her to the church, and you'll be perfect, Henry.'

'But what about the petrol?' asked Bubble.

'Petrol doesn't matter for weddings,' said Morris.

'Cool,' said Bubble.

'Well done, Morris,' said Auntie Rover.

Henry wanted to do the wedding, but what would Mr Fettler say? Anxiously he watched as Mr Fettler walked over. He shook from his bonnet to his chassis.

'Well, hurry up, Henry,' said Mr Fettler. 'Go and have a wash and polish.'

Later that afternoon the bells at the church rang out. The cars of Cosy Park Garage crammed into the doorway to watch out for the bride. Even Mr Fettler was there. They saw the bridesmaids go by. Time passed and Morris began to feel worried. Where was Henry?

'Woof,' barked Dog. His sharp ears could hear 'Kathonka kathonka kathonka'. Henry was on his way. And, at last, there he was, at the end of their long road, slowly driving nearer and nearer.

Henry looked magnificent, with white ribbons tied from his silver radiator to his gleaming windscreen. The sun reflected from his polished bonnet. The bride sat in the back like a fairy princess.

Prince Henry's sad old heart glowed with pride – at least his final drive was a very special occasion. All his friends cheered as he drove by. They watched his stately progress past until he disappeared round the corner on his way to the church.

Henry had enjoyed his day very much, but that evening, back in Cosy Park Garage, at his place by the stove, once more he felt very sad. How could he bear to be sent away from his friends and be shut away forever in the lonely museum.

'Cheer up Henry,' said Mr Fettler. 'You did so well today it has given me a great idea. You can stay at Cosy Park Garage after all, and be our wedding car.'

Everyone cheered, and Henry glowed with joy. His big old engine filled up to the brim with love for his wonderful friends.

© Mal Leicester & Roger Twelvetrees

Cars have gradually developed from the clumsy beginnings of Nicolas Cugnot's steam carriage of 1769 (Figure 6.6), through:

the 'horseless carriage' era of the 1880s and 1890s (notice how the 1893 Benz Victoria, Figure 6.7 looks just like a carriage with no horses);

the Edwardian era of stately grandeur (Figure 6.8, 1907 Rolls Royce Silver Ghost) – see how high the passengers sit to gaze upon the common people below; and

the elegance of the 'golden age' of the 1920s and 1930s, when cars were often pieces of art (Figure 6.9 1937 Alvis Speed 25);

into a jelly mould shape that is primarily a cost-effective way of getting from 'A to B'.

Sources of graphics:

FIGURE 6.6 (Cugnot steam tractor): http://en.wikipedia.org/wiki/Nicolas-Joseph_Cugnot, http://en.wikipedia.org/wiki/File:Fardier_a_vapeur.gif

FIGURE 6.7 (1893 Benz Victoria): http://upload.wikimedia.org/wikipedia/commons/7/71/1885Benz.jpg

FIGURE 6.8 (1907 Rolls Royce Silver Ghost): http://upload.wikimedia.org/wikipedia/commons/a/a2/Rolls-Royce_Silver_Ghost_at_Centenary.jpg

FIGURE 6.9 (1937 Alvis): http://en.wikipedia.org/wiki/Alvis_Cars http://wapedia.mobi/thumb/9d9214699/en/max/1440/900/1937-alvis-automobile-archives.jpg?format=jpg,png,gif&loadexternal=1

FIGURE 6.10 (Smart car): http://en.wikipedia.org/wiki/File:Nuvola-blue-smart-fortwo-2.jpg

7

Brave Grace Darling

An adventure at sea

Topics and themes

The boy-friendly topic for this chapter is a daring sea rescue and the universal theme is courage. The story is a fictionalised account of a real-life heroine and is another story in the collection which features a heroine rather than a hero. The resources provide transport-related activities, and learning activities which include boats, trains and planes.

Literacy development

Introduce the story vocabulary in your usual way.

Read the story yourself but vary subsequent readings – the children reading aloud in turn or reading to themselves.

Talking about the story and the literacy activities provided aim to develop oracy, reading skills and practice in a variety of writing forms.

Subject areas

Geography, History, ICT

Cross-curricular values

Courage

Interdisciplinary projects

Transport

Suggested resources

Two photocopiable pages are provided

Books

Fiction

Illustrated Stories for Boys, various authors (Usborne)
The Lighthouse Boy: A Story About Courage, R. H. Schneider (Richard H. Schneider and Anton Petrov)

Non-fiction

Transport: The Amazing Story of Ships, Trains, Aircraft and Cars, and How They Work, P. Mellett and C. Oxlade (Lorenz Books)
Transport Around the World: Pack A, C. Oxlade (Heinemann Library)
The Boys' Book of Model Aeroplanes: How to Build and Fly Them, F. A. Collins (The Century Co.)
Lighthouses for Kids, K. L. House (Chicago Review Press)

Web sites

www.rnli.org.uk/who_we_are/the_heritage_trust/grace-darling-museum
www.svr.co.uk/education.php
www.nps.gov/history/Nr/twhp/wwwlps/lessons/111wrightoh/111facts1.htm
timeline: http://memory.loc.gov/ammem/wrighthtml/wrighttime.html

Vocabulary

Lighthouse	A house on rocks out to sea or on a cliff top, with a bright light on top to warn ships
Fierce	With high winds and driving rain
Battering	Crashing against
Intently	Concentrating on one thing
Tense	Stressed, alert and ready to move quickly
Survivors	People not drowned
Frail	Not strong
Jagged	Sharp edged and irregular
Struggle	Use all one's strength to achieve one's aim
Reef	A line of rocks

Rescued	Brought to safety
Remaining	Those left behind
Tended	Looked after
Courage	Being able to do something really dangerous in a calm way
Heroine	A female who has displayed courage in helping others in distress and is honoured for it

The story

Brave Grace Darling

Grace Darling lived on the Farne Islands with her mother and father. Her father was the Longstone Lighthouse keeper. Grace enjoyed living in the lighthouse. On fine days she liked watching the sea and the great sailing ships. On wet days she liked the rainy sounds. Sometimes she would do her needlework, warm and cosy by the wood stove in the large ground-floor living room.

One September night when she was twenty-three years old, a fierce storm blew up, battering the lighthouse walls with huge waves. Grace lay awake listening to the storm and worrying about any ships caught in it. As the hours crawled by she slept fitfully. She drifted in and out of sleep, always waking to the sound of the howling wind and crashing water.

In the early hours of the morning Grace took her turn looking out from the top of the lighthouse. She had not been there long when she thought she saw something in the sea, being battered about by huge waves. She peered through the darkness. *It must be the wreck of a ship*, she thought. For a long time she watched the black shape, waiting for the dawn so that she could see it more clearly. Gradually the darkness grew lighter. Grace, frowning out even more intently, grew still and tense. Surely something had moved on Big Harcar rock. Through narrowed eyes Grace stared and stared until she was sure. There were survivors out there!

Grace hurried for her father who came and saw for himself.

'The storm is too strong for the North Sunderland Lifeboat to come out here,' he said, half to himself. 'I'll have to row out to the rock myself.'

'You can't manage alone, father,' Grace said. 'I'll come too.'

Grace's father did not like this idea, but there was no one else to help him. He looked again at the survivors, clinging to the rock.

'Wrap up warm, and bring blankets,' he said.

Grace and her father set out, their rowing boat small and frail in the raging sea. Grace kept a look out for the jagged rocks which could wreck them while her father rowed and rowed. It was a long, cold, scary mile to Big Harcar, but at last they reached the survivors.

William Darling leapt out of his boat to help them. Now Grace had to struggle on her own to keep from being smashed on the reef. She used every ounce of strength she had rowing backwards and forwards to keep the

FIGURE 7.1 Grace Darling.

boat in one place. Grace's father helped a woman and an injured man into the boat. Three other men clambered aboard, taking over the rowing for the journey back to the lighthouse. The small boat was full. Grace comforted the woman whose two children has drowned in the sea. The light of Longstone Lighthouse slowly came nearer and was a comfort to Grace herself.

Once back, Grace helped the woman and the injured man into the warm living room.

'There are four men still on the rock,' said Grace's father.

He chose two of the rescued men to row back with him and fetch the remaining survivors.

With her mother Grace tended the injured man and the grieving woman, though part of her mind went with her father, longing for his safe return. She felt a huge relief when he arrived back with his two helpers and all the remaining survivors.

'We did it,' he said to Grace, giving her a hug. 'With our small rowing boat and your huge courage, Grace, this night we have saved nine souls.'

Later William Darling and his daughter were awarded with gold and silver medals. Even Queen Victoria sent Grace fifty pounds. Grace never sought this attention but she became a famous heroine and has been honoured for her courage from that day to this – for over 170 years.

© Mal Leicester

Literacy development

Talking about the story

- Where did Grace Darling live?

- What did she see at dawn after a stormy night?

- What could have wrecked her small boat?

- How did she keep the boat in one place?

- Who did she and her father save on the first journey?

- What did Queen Victoria send Grace?

Points for discussion

- What did Grace like about living in the lighthouse?

- Why couldn't she sleep that September night?

- Why is Grace regarded as a heroine?

- Explain that the lifeboat service is manned by unpaid volunteers. Why do you think that people are willing to risk their lives doing this dangerous job?

Literacy activities

KS1

The children draw their own story entitled 'Storm at Sea'.

KS2

The children write their own story entitled 'Storm at Sea'.

For gifted or enthusiastic children

What can the children find out about Grace Darling which is not already contained in the fictionalised story ('Brave Grace Darling')? They should use the school ICT suite and the school or local library.

Subject-centred activities

Geography

Explain to the children that a lighthouse is there to warn ships of rocks at that part of the coast. Show the children the Farne Islands on Ordnance Survey map sheet 75. Show them the small lighthouse symbol showing Longstone Lighthouse. Show the children the map of lighthouses around the coast of the UK (web site: www.trinityhouse.co.uk/lighthouse_review_map/index.html). Divide the class into small groups and let each group choose a stretch of coast with several lighthouses, for example round St David's Head in Pembrokeshire, or round Land's End in Cornwall. Each group is given the OS sheet for that piece of coast and the children copy the coast line and rocks and show the lighthouse symbols in the correct places. This could be a good starting point for finding out about ports, towns, sea and land communications in the area. Older children might enjoy the informative BBC programme *Coast*.

History/ICT

Give the children photocopiable pages 99–100.

The Wright brothers provide a striking example of inventive creativity. Use the information sheets about the amazing Wright brothers as a class read.

The children use the schools ICT suite to obtain information to construct a timeline for either aviation or locomotives.

Cross-curricular values

Courage: let each child choose a real-life hero or heroine. You could encourage some of the children to choose a local hero. Try to ensure a variety of types of hero and or different kinds of courage. Once more using the school ICT suite and the school or local library the children should find out more about their chosen person. They should write a brief account of what their hero/heroine did/achieved and comment on why this was a brave and courageous deed. They could also draw a picture of the courageous scene. The written accounts alternating with the accompanying picture could make an interesting frieze along one classroom wall.

Interdisciplinary topic

Transport

Many teachers will have already used transport as an interesting and interdisciplinary topic. The work in this chapter will have complemented and reinforced such work.

To bring it all together focus with the children on the advantages and disadvantages of the various modes of travel, on foot, by bicycle, by boat, by train, by car, by plane.

First brainstorm with the children some advantages and disadvantages of each of the above.

Move on to consider the relative advantages and disadvantages; for example, ask the children which of the following they prefer and why.

1   Going a very long way by car but with plenty of stops for picnics etc.

2   Going the same distance on an overnight train when you can sleep for part of the journey

3   Going for the same distance by plane without breaks or sleep but in a much shorter time

Finally, in their own exercise books let the children take each form of transport (on foot, by bicycle, by boat, by train, by car, by plane) and write down what they consider to be the three strongest advantages and the three strongest disadvantages.

The amazing Wright brothers

Wilbur and Orville Wright were the sons of Milton Wright, a bishop of the United Brethren in Christ. Wilbur was born in 1867 and Orville four years later. They were inseparable, their personalities perfectly complementing each other. Orville was full of ideas and enthusiasms while Wilbur was more steady in his habits, more mature in his judgements, and more likely to see a project through.

Their parents supported and encouraged the boys' inventiveness by providing a stimulating home. Their mother provided the mechanical expertise and their father the intellectual challenge. Milton brought them various souvenirs and trinkets he found during his travels for the church and Susan, their mother, showed them how they worked and how to mend them if they broke. The boys came to love playing with anything mechanical and investigating how it worked. Their toys included a gyroscope, an old sewing machine and a small helicopter-like toy operated by rubber bands. The latter is what sparked their interest in flying machines.

In later life, Orville said, 'We were lucky enough to grow up in a home environment where there was always much encouragement to children to pursue intellectual interests; to investigate whatever aroused curiosity. In a different kind of environment our curiosity might have been nipped long before it could have borne fruit.'

At a young age, Wilbur, to earn pocket money, took on a job of folding an entire issue of an eight-page church paper. However, the work became too tedious and tiring, so Wilbur invented a machine to do the folding for him. Likewise Orville earned money by designing his own kites that he made and sold.

The brothers' first joint project was the building of a two-metre-long treadle-powered wood lathe. The lathe was a complex project and not without its teething troubles, one of which became the talk of the neighbourhood.

Nowadays lathes run quietly on steel ball bearings, but in the nineteenth century ball bearings were far too expensive for the young Wright brothers. They could however get marbles, so they decided to use marbles to make the spindle bearings instead. Glass marbles were quite expensive too, so they decided to try clay marbles instead. While Wilbur was gleefully trying out his exciting new machine on high speed the clay bearings started to disintegrate, causing a great roaring noise and shaking the whole lathe. At the same time Orville, who was approaching the shed downhill on his bike, lost control and crashed heavily into the shed, causing it to shake. Wilbur thought this must be an earthquake and rushed out of the shed in panic expecting it to collapse at any second.

Adventure Stories for Reading, Learning and Literacy, Routledge © Mal Leicester and Roger Twelvetrees, 2010

In school Wilbur excelled, and he would have graduated from high school if his family had not moved during his senior year. (Later a sporting accident and his mother's illness and subsequent death kept him from going to Yale and then entering the clergy.) Orville was an average student known for his mischievous behaviour, which led to an expulsion, and he quit school altogether before his final year.

As soon as Orville was clear of school he and Wilbur set up a printing business using a press that they built themselves from a damaged gravestone and parts from a horse-drawn cart. They did odd jobs for others and printed their own newspaper.

In the 1890s the 'safety cycle', which looks much like the bicycle of today, was taking over from the 'penny farthing' and in 1892 the brothers bought bicycles. They began repairing bicycles for friends and soon set up their own repair business. In 1893 the shop began selling new bicycles and three years later they were selling their own designs of bicycle.

In 1896 Orville fell ill with typhoid, and while Wilbur was nursing him he read of the exploits of European aviation pioneers who were trying to build the first successful 'heavier than air' aircraft. This led him to take an interest in flying and he began in 1899 by obtaining all the research papers that the American Smithsonian Institution could supply.

Only four years later, one Saturday afternoon in 1903, Wilbur and Orville Wright made final repairs and adjustments to their aircraft. On Thursday, 17 December, 1903, Wilbur and Orville achieved their goal—the world's first powered flight. Orville flew the Wright Flyer a distance of about thirty-seven metres (120 feet), staying aloft for twelve seconds. Later the same day, Wilbur flew about 260 metres (852 feet) in a flight lasting fifty-nine seconds.

This was the high point of the brothers' intense study and research on the principles of flight. Along the way they had built their own wind tunnel, carried out their own basic research on aerofoils, made the first successful piloted glider, designed the first successful propeller and aero engine and developed the basic layout of the aeroplane that we see today.

8

Boy racer

Topics and themes

The boy-friendly topic for this chapter is car racing and the universal theme is friendship. The story is about a boy who dreams of becoming a racing driver but finds his friendship is even more important. The resources provide exciting racing-related activities, and classroom learning about friendship.

Literacy development

Introduce the story vocabulary in your usual way.

Read the story yourself but vary subsequent readings – the children reading aloud in turn or reading to themselves.

Talking about the story and the literacy activities provided aim to develop oracy, reading skills and practice in a variety of writing forms.

Subject areas

Maths, Science, Art

Cross-curricular values

Friendship

Interdisciplinary projects

Road safety

Suggested resources

Seven photocopiable pages are provided

Books

Fiction

CARS

Racing Cars, P. Worms (Motormania)
Boy Racer (Books for Boys), I. Whybrow and A. Ross (Hodder)

FRIENDSHIP

The Hundred Dresses, E. Estes and L. Slobodkin (Harcourt)
Because of Winn-Dixie, K. Di Camillo (Walker)

Non-fiction

Top Gear: The Official Annual 2010, anon. (BBC Children's Books)
Cars (Transport around the World), C. Oxlade (Heinemann)

Web sites

www.karting.co.uk/
www.formula1.com/
www.lemans.org/24heuresdumans/pages/accueil_gb.html

Vocabulary

Sledge	A long seat with runners underneath that runs on snow
Nervous	Worried
Focussed	Concentrated on one thing and ignored what was happening around him
Matched	Almost the same
Annual	Once a year
Funding	Money to pay for things
Expensive	Requiring a lot of money
Competitive	Really wanting to come first
Congratulate	Tell someone, 'well done'

Regret   Wish you had not done something
Quit   No longer take part
Confide   Tell someone something in secret
Wiry   Thin but strong
Progress   Getting better at doing something
Impressed   Made someone see you are very good at something

Racing-related vocabulary

Speed   How fast a car goes
Fastest   The one who passes all the others
Go-kart   Simple very small car with four small wheels and an exposed engine
Starting grid   Where the drivers line up for the start of the race
Overtaking   Going past
Championship   A series of races in which drivers score points. The champion has the most points in the year
Formula 1 World The Formula 1 driver with the most points at the end of the
  Champion   year
Revved up   Excited, high engine speed
Lapping   Overtaking other cars for the second time, i.e. more than one lap of the track ahead
Finishing line Where the race finishes, usually also the start line

The story

Boy racer

Ever since Davy could remember he had loved speed. He was always the fastest racer on his bike and the fastest down snowy hills on his sledge. For his eighth birthday Mum and Dad bought him a go-kart. He was thrilled.

Davy's house had its own long drive up to and around the large garden. Davy practised there until he drove his go-kart really well. One day his dad said, 'You're confident enough to drive at the kart racing track now,' and he took Davy and his kart there that weekend. Davy was nervous making his way with the other racers to the starting grid. Most of the others were older than he was and had obviously raced before but once the flag fell Davy focussed on driving his fastest. He wanted to be at the front and was soon confidently overtaking the others. He crossed the line first, winning the race.

'Well done,' said the boy who had come second. 'I'm Josh.'

The two boys chatted over a juice.

'My problem is I have nowhere to practise,' Josh said.

'He can come over to our house, can't he?' Davy asked Dad.

After that, twice a week Josh came over and he and Davy raced round the driveway. They used cones to vary the track and sometimes Davy won and sometimes Josh. They were well matched and became very good friends.

The following year the boys entered the British Formula Cadet Kart Championship. Over the year they each won several times. Davy was the youngest driver ever to win a round.

Later Davy and Josh started entering the British Open Kart Championships and again each had success. Davy won in the first year, once more the youngest ever. Josh won the following year.

'One day I'll be Formula 1 World Champion,' vowed Davy.

'And one day I will too,' said Josh.

Some years later Davy and Josh entered the annual young driver event. The prize included funding to support a promising young driver and a test in a McLaren Formula 1 car. This would be a way of being noticed by the Formula 1 team bosses.

Davy was revved up with excitement and determination. He had never wanted to win more strongly than he did that day. Just before the race he

FIGURE 8.1 Go-kart racing.

and Josh met up. Davy could tell that Josh was worried. He was not just hyped up for the race but worried too.

'What's up, mate?' Davy said.

'Oh, nothing really.'

'Come on, you can tell me.'

'Well, Dad's business is going down. This is my last chance. If I don't win and get that funding Dad can't support my racing any more.'

'I'm sorry, Josh,' said Davy. He knew that racing was expensive and that he was lucky to have a well-off Dad.

The race began and Josh roared ahead of the field. Davy stayed a close second, knowing he could increase his speed later in the race. The two boys were soon lapping the rest. Davy's blood was fizzing with excitement and coming to the final lap he overtook Josh and knew he was going to win.

Josh's words came into Davy's mind. *This is my last chance.* Suddenly, against all his competitive feelings, he slowed, just enough to allow Josh to whiz by and cross the finishing line first.

Davy watched everyone throng around Josh to congratulate him. He knew he must do so too.

'Well done Josh,' Davy said, forcing a smile.

It was hard to watch Josh receive his award. *That should have been me*, Davy thought and he couldn't tell anyone, even Josh, what he had done. Davy didn't regret it, though. It would have been even harder to watch his friend be forced to quit racing because he, Davy, had won.

Later, when he and his Dad were packing up to go home he wondered whether to confide in his Dad, who couldn't help looking disappointed about the race. Before Davy could decide a messenger arrived to ask them to go to Ron Williams's motor-home in the paddock. Ron Williams was a Formula 1 team boss. He was a wiry and energetic man, with piecing eyes and a stern face that relaxed into a wide friendly smile when he met them. He gave them coffee.

'You could have won that race young man. I want to know why you didn't.'

Davy looked into the unblinking blue eyes, bright as headlights, and knew that this man could not be fooled. He told him the truth about Josh.

'I thought so! Davy, if you promise me never to pull back again, then I'll promise you that I'll watch your progress with a view to a place on my team.' He put out his hand and raised his eyebrows questioningly.

Davy and Ron Williams shook hands.

'I promise,' said Davy.

On the way home Dad was rather quiet. Davy wondered if he was angry about the lost race.

'Are you mad at me, Dad?'

'Mad at you! said Dad, 'Absolutely not. The reverse. I am proud of you son. The best and youngest driver and a true friend to Josh. And you've impressed Ron Williams and will get your chance. Mum will be proud of you too. I've never been more sure than I am today that you'll follow your dream and become the Formula 1 World Champion. Just think of that, Davy – champion of the whole world.'

© Mal Leicester

Literacy development

Talking about the story

- What did Davy get for his birthday?

- How often did Josh come to Davy's house for practice?

- In the story who was the youngest ever British Open Kart Champion?

- Why did Josh need to win the annual young driver event?

- What did Davy do for his friend?

- What did Davy promise Ron Williams?

Points for discussion

- Davy's dream was to be a Formula 1 champion. What dreams do the children have?

- Do you think Davy was right to let Josh win?

- How do you think that Ron Williams knew that Davy threw the race? (The children may say that through his experience he could tell he pulled back. This is a good answer, but you could also tell them that he would know from the lap times, which are recorded.)

- The plot of the story involves a lost race, but ask the children what else the story is about. (The theme. There is no one correct answer. They might say, determination, practising, racing or friendship etc.)

Literacy activities

KS1: Story and sequencing

Give the children photocopiable pages 117–118. They must choose the correct caption for each picture. They can place these under the picture by writing them in (i.e. copying the sentences) or you could photocopy the sentences onto sticky labels.

KS2

The children can write their own story entitled 'The Race'. Can the children remember races in any of the other stories in this collection? ('The Long Swim' has a race between Alpha and the pike, 'Terror in the Tunnel' has a race between the twins and the bombers, 'Percy's Big Adventure' has a race between Percy and Balilla. There is a kind of race against time to capture the evil ghost in 'The Evil Ghost of Castle Chameleon'.) For their own story, the children will decide who is racing and why and if it is a real race or perhaps a race against time.

Subject-centred activities

Maths

Arithmetic using speed

On land to measure walking speed we can measure out a mile on the ground and then time how long it takes for a person to walk along that piece of ground. If it takes a person one hour to walk that mile then they are travelling at one mile per hour. If it takes half an hour to travel the mile then the person could go two miles in one whole hour so speed is 2 mph. There are sixty minutes in an hour, so if the person got into a car and drove the mile in one minute then the car could travel sixty miles in a full hour, so the speed is 60 mph.

If it takes you fifteen minutes to walk a mile, how many miles will you walk in an hour?

If a snail crawls half a mile in a week how long will it need to crawl a mile?

If a hare can run at thirty miles per hour how far can it run in three hours?

NB: You could construct more of these arithmetic problems and the children might enjoy the story of the hare and the tortoise.

We don't have to measure out a full mile to find the speed. Have you noticed the markings on the road near GATSO speed cameras? There the speed is measured over quite a short distance. We can (for instance) measure how fast you can walk and run by measuring our speed over a distance of one hundredth of a mile and then multiplying that time by 100 to get the time it would take you to cover one mile.

Speed measurement

Measure out a distance of 16 m 9 cm (1/100 mile) outside in the yard or the sports field or, if the weather is foul, inside in a gym or other large space. Choose two tall children to walk along the measured 1/100 mile. Choose two more children to act as observers at the start and end of the measured 1/100 mile. Set yourself up with the stop watch yourself, or if any of the class are sufficiently skilled ask them to do it. The children doing the walk are to walk side by side, keeping in step from a few metres before the measured 1/100 mile to a few metres after the end. As they cross the start line the first observer raises his/her hand and as they cross the finishing line the second observer raises his/her hand. Write the time in seconds on the board and repeat the exercise a few times to get a consistent result. (The teacher is to calculate the speed in mph: add two noughts to get the time in seconds to cover a mile at that speed, and then divide by the number of seconds in an hour (3600) to get the speed in mph). Write the speed in mph alongside the time in seconds.

Repeat the exercise a few times with the pair running together and in step along the measured 1/100 mile. Repeat with other pairs of children and other observers. The teacher is to use the calculator to work out the speed and write it on the board, then work out with the calculator how much faster running is than walking. Express to the children as twice or almost one and a half times etc.

How fast does a car go in town? (30 mph.) How many times faster is that than the walking and running speeds of children? Teacher work out with the calculator but round up/down to the nearest whole number and write on the board.

How fast does a car go on a motorway? (70 mph.) How many times faster is that than the walking and running speeds of children? Teacher work out with the calculator but round up/down to the nearest whole number and write on the board.

How fast does a train go? (~125 mph.) How many times faster is that than the walking and running speeds of children? Work out with the calculator but round up/down to the nearest whole number and write on the board.

How fast does a normal passenger plane go? (~500 mph.) How many times faster is that than the walking and running speeds of children? Work out with the calculator but round up/down to the nearest whole number, write on the board and discuss with the class.

The children can enjoy free play while waiting for their turn.

Science

Ask the children to bring in some Dinky cars.

With the children make some ramps of differing heights. Let the children 'play' with the cars and ramps, noticing how much faster they can make the cars go with a steeper slope.

Art

Seeing and drawing speed

How can we tell a car is going fast on the road? (It zooms by.) How can we tell if a car in a photograph is going fast? (Sometimes it is blurred but we may not be able to tell.) How can we tell if a car in a painting is going fast? (Perhaps if it's an open car the driver has a scarf that is blowing in the wind, perhaps the watching spectators are shown blurred, perhaps there are lines from the wheels or edges of the car to show speed.) If possible have some images of racing cars to show the children. Now the children can draw their own racing car, trying to create an impression of speed in their own picture. The best of these could be mounted on the classroom wall.

Cross-curricular values

Friendship

We all need friends, and a child who is friendless at school, even if not actively bullied, won't be a happy child. Try to match such children in classroom activities with other lonely or new or kindly children. The following activities do not assume that every child has a friend!

Making friends

With the children brainstorm some out-of-school clubs that children can join (for example, Cubs, badminton, chess).

Pen friends

Perhaps you could link your pupils to children of a similar age in another school, giving each child a pen friend. They could write their first letter in class introducing themselves.

A good friend

With the children brainstorm the qualities of a good friend. (For example, sharing, understanding, fun to play with.)

A pretend friend

Let the children draw a picture of a pretend friend and write a descriptive piece about the person: their name and age, their appearance, their personality, why I like them. Remind the children to find some strong adjectives for their descriptions.

Interdisciplinary activities

Road safety

1   Brainstorm with the children what speed could be considered good (e.g. useful – plane travel – or pleasurable – galloping a horse, sledging down a hill on snow, watching a motor race).

2   Read the photocopiable story 'Bubble Trouble'. Brainstorm with the children what speed could be considered bad (e.g. going too fast on the road and causing an accident, running along a slippery corridor).

3   Go over the six points from the Green Cross Code concerning crossing a road safely. It is important the children understand these, and you could practise in the school playground or gym.

- Find a safe place to cross, then stop

- Stand on the pavement near the kerb

- Look all around for traffic and listen

- If traffic is coming, let it pass – look all around again

- When there is no traffic near, walk straight across the road

- Keep looking and listening for traffic while you cross

4   You can find useful road safety games on the following web sites:

- www.roadsafetyweek.org/educators/web-centre/in-the-classroom/websites-for-primary-school-children

- www.dft.gov.uk/think/focusareas/children/?whoareyou_id=

- www.familylearning.org.uk/road_safety_games.html

5   This is a good topic for a visiting speaker such as a community policeman or a road safety officer.

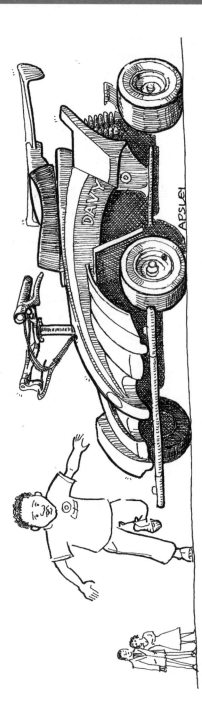

FIGURE 8.2 Mum and Dad give Davy a go-kart.

Bubble trouble
Book Two in the Cosy Park Garage Series

'Now, young Bubble,' Mr Fettler said, 'can you do an errand all by yourself?'

'Oh yes, Mr Fettler,' said Bubble, revving his engine with excitement.

'Splendid. Landie needs a new battery. In this cold weather, his engine might not start on the old one. You can go to Car World and get it for him.'

Impatient to be off, Bubble revved his engine even louder.

'Now listen, Bubble, I'm trusting you. Don't let me down . . . or Landie. And watch your speed, lad. Mind that corner at the bottom of High Cliff Hill.'

Bubble wasn't listening. Straining to be off, he charged out of Cosy Park Garage like a racing car.

Auntie Rover and Landie looked at each other.

'I fear the worst,' said Auntie Rover.

Bubble tore along, his engine singing, enjoying every moment.

'Faster faster faster,' he shouted. He stormed up to the top of High Cliff Hill.

'Look at me, look at me,' he roared. He hurtled down, still at full speed, beeping his horn.

'Beep beep beep.'

He was almost at the bottom of the hill when, sick with sudden terror, he realised he was going much too fast for the corner. Out of control, he careered off the road, hurtling towards a stone gatepost. Bubble screamed, and closed his headlights waiting for the crash. He missed the post by a whisker, but now found himself bouncing over a bumpy field heading straight for a pond.

'Help,' he shouted.

The water looked deep and dark and dangerous. Bubble slid down a steep bank and with a bump and a splash came to a stop. His engine was thudding hard and his front wheels were up to their axles in the pond.

I'm in really bad trouble now, thought Bubble. *I can't drive forward through the deeper water, and I've no reverse gear to back out. I'm stuck.* A large cow stared at Bubble and gave an angry moo. Bubble was frightened. It was growing dark. *I will be stuck here all night and Mr Fettler will be so cross with me.* He strained his headlights to keep a watch on the horses, and the cows

FIGURE 8.3 Bubble shooting through the farm gate.

and the foxes coming down to the pond for a drink. He was scared one of them might bite his tyres. The hoot of an owl made him jump.

I'm sinking deeper into the mud and if it gets into my engine I'll never drive again. Bubble trembled with fear. He felt the mud rising up his wheels. *It might go right over my roof and I'll never be found.*

Bubble had given up hope of rescue when he heard a sound which he recognised. His engine gave a leap of joy. It was the scream of Landie's transfer gearbox. But then Bubble heard him driving away. He started to sob. *He can't see me. I'll be stuck here for ever, and it's all my own fault.* Bubble's tears plopped heavily into the muddy pond and made ripples that lapped up his wheels.

A few moments later he heard Morris coming down the hill, his engine purring like a cat. *Please Morris, don't go past,* thought Bubble, *please please Morris.*

To Bubble's joy he heard Morris bumping over the field towards him.

How did he know where I am? Bubble wondered.

'Woof,' he heard. 'Woof woof Bubble.'

Dog had followed his scent as dogs do, and Morris had followed Dog.

'Oh Morris, Morris,' choked Bubble, tears pouring down his headlights. 'I'm so glad to see you. Please get me out of here.'

'I can't,' said Morris, 'but Landie can.'

'Landie's gone past,' wailed Bubble.

'Don't worry Bubble, I'll go and bring him back,' said Morris.

'Please don't leave me on my own, Morris.'

'Don't worry, Bubble. Dog will stay and look after you.'

'Woof,' agreed Dog, wagging his tail.

'I've let them down, Dog,' sighed Bubble. 'I didn't even collect the battery for Landie and it's all my fault for going too fast. I should have listened to Mr Fettler. He'll never trust me out on my own again.'

Dog put his head on Bubble's bonnet to comfort him.

Before long Morris returned with Landie.

'I need to reverse behind Bubble, ready to pull him up the bank,' said Landie. They had brought a tow rope, which had a loop at each end. Dog dropped one loop on Bubble's rear bumper and the other on Landie's recovery hook. Landie began to pull, but instead of tightening the rope, his engine coughed and stopped.

'I'd forget my head if it wasn't bolted down,' said Landie. 'I forgot to put my gearbox into low ratio. I'll try again.'

But Landie's engine wouldn't start up. It coughed and wheezed like an old man.

'It's my old battery,' Landie said. 'I'll turn my headlights off and let it rest for ten minutes and then try again.'

For what seemed a very long time Bubble waited and waited and waited. *If only I'd got his new battery*, he thought anxiously. At last he heard Landie try his engine once more. He heard the engine groan and groan again. When he heard it fire up he gave a cry of relief.

Landie carefully put his gearbox in low-ratio four-wheel drive and again began to pull. Bubble could see Morris and Dog watching anxiously and he felt his bumper being pulled very very hard.

'My bumper will break right off,' he yelled to Landie, just as he began to move backwards millimetre by millimetre out of the pond.

'Hurray!' they all shouted.

Soon Bubble was driving home behind Morris and Landie. All his friends at Cosy Park were pleased to see them. Everyone was smiling except Mr Fettler, who gave Bubble a stern telling off.

Adventure Stories for Reading, Learning and Literacy, Routledge © Mal Leicester and Roger Twelvetrees, 2010

'You could have crashed into the gatepost or drowned your engine in the pond. You would have finished up in Bad End Scrap Yard, and serve you right,' he raged.

Bubble hung his bonnet in shame.

'Don't worry, Bubble,' whispered Morris when Mr Fettler had gone back to his office. 'He'll give you another chance.'

'And I'll never let him down again, Morris,' promised Bubble.

Morris smiled and at last Bubble smiled back. Mr Fettler would forgive him and he was very happy to be safely home.

© Mal Leicester and Roger Twelvetrees

Bubble, do not go too fast, says Mr Fettler.

Bubble goes fast. He lands in a pond.

A big cow scares Bubble.

Dog finds Bubble.

Dog brings Landie.
Landie pulls Bubble out of the pond.

Bubble is happy. He goes home with his friends.